POPULAR
CULTURE
REVIEW

· ·

volume 33 number 2 fall 2022

Amy M. Green, editor-in-chief

Westphalia Press
An Imprint of the Policy Studies Organization
Washington, DC
2022

Popular Culture Review gratefully acknowledges the contributions and support by the University of Nevada, Las Vegas: College of Liberal Arts, and the University of Nevada, Las Vegas: Department of English.

POPULAR CULTURE REVIEW: Vol. 33, No. 2, Fall 2022

Westphalia Press
An imprint of Policy Studies Organization
1367 Connecticut Ave NW
Washington, D.C. 20036
info@ipsonet.org

ISBN: 978-1-63723-826-4

Table of Contents

. . . .

SPECIAL ISSUE 33.2 COVID-19 AND POPULAR CULTURE

Editor's Note

· · · · · · · · · · · · · · · · · · ·

This Special Issue focuses on how COVID-19 impacted our popular culture, from popular culture offerings themselves to how we might consume them. The articles in this issue provide diverse considerations of this impact.

Kimberly Owczarski explores the overall change in moviegoing during the pandemic and how movie theater chains, with a specific focus on AMC, have been pivoting to adapt to these fundamental shifts.

Tyler Johnson and Lisa Funnell explore the specific impact of COVID-19 on the release of the newest James Bond film, *No Time to Die.* It is an excellent companion piece to Owczarski's article, as these authors consider moviegoing from two different perspectives.

Anna Marini and Michael Fuchs explore a different aspect of the pandemic, in the form of images in the music and music videos by the metal band Cattle Decapitation. Michael Fuchs published an article in *Popular Culture Review* recently titled "'A Serious Man Versus Nature Moment:' Aquatic Monsters, Deep Time, and Climate Change."

Shelly Galliah considers John Oliver's television presence and how, as a result of the pandemic, he took on a role as a science journalist. Over the course of the pandemic, Oliver's program increasingly served to refute misinformation and junk science.

Vicky Pettersen Lantz provides an analysis of how Disney World coped with aspects of the pandemic like social distancing. She considers how the theme mark demarcated spaces and changed exhibitions during this time.

Finally, Sarah Breyfogle considers the production of fan fiction in her article, and the ways in which the authors of fan fiction worked through the cultural trauma of the last few years. Her work with fan fiction dovetails well with the interview in the last issue with Anna Wilson.

This issue also marks the return of book reviews. The two reviews published in this issue reflect the diversity of writing in the popular culture realm. Madison Kooba reviews the experimental fiction work *Protectress,* while Carlos Tkacz reviews *Pop Culture Freaks,* which focuses on mass media and culture.

I am proud to share with you the compelling and engaging work published in this issue.

Dr. Amy M. Green, Editor, *Popular Culture Review*

Toward a "New Normal": A Case Study of the Pandemic's Effect on Film Exhibition

....

By Kimberly Owczarski

ABSTRACT

As the largest theatrical chain globally, AMC Theatres faced enormous financial losses during the coronavirus pandemic, but the company also found opportunities to expand their business and contest the studios' growing dependence on streaming services. AMC provides a case study of how the pandemic affected movie theaters and how chains negotiated this challenging time. AMC's ability to overcome these challenges provides a blueprint for what it takes to survive in the theatrical business moving forward.

Keywords: COVID-19, Film Exhibition, AMC Theaters

RESUMEN

Como la cadena de cines más grande del mundo, AMC Theatres enfrentó enormes pérdidas financieras durante la pandemia de coronavirus, pero la compañía también encontró oportunidades para expandir su negocio y desafiar la creciente dependencia de los estudios de los servicios de transmisión. AMC ofrece un estudio de caso de cómo la pandemia afectó a las salas de cine y cómo las cadenas negociaron este momento difícil. La capacidad de AMC para superar estos desafíos proporciona un modelo de lo que se necesita para sobrevivir en el futuro del negocio teatral.

Palabras clave: COVID-19, Exhibición de Cine, AMC Theatres

迈向'新常态'：将大流行对电影展产生的影响作为案例研究

摘要

作为全球最大的电影院线，AMC电影院在2019冠状病毒病大流行期间面临巨大的财务损失，但该公司也找到了机会扩大业务并减少对流媒体服务日益增长的依赖。AMC为研究大流行如何影响电影院以及院线如何度过这一困难时期提供了案例。AMC在克服这些挑战方面具备的能力为今后电影业务的生存条件提供了蓝图。

关键词：2019冠状病毒病，电影展，AMC电影院

On March 11, 2020, the National Association of Theater Owners (NATO) announced the cancellation of the upcoming CinemaCon, the annual event where studios extravagantly promote their upcoming features to theater owners from around the world. In a statement, NATO stressed that "While local outbreaks [of coronavirus] vary widely in severity, the global circumstances make it impossible for us to mount the show that our attendees have come to expect" (Donnelly). The cancellation was due to the rapid increase of coronavirus cases globally, particularly the growing number in the United States. The event's cancellation signaled the start of the COVID-19 pandemic's effect on movie exhibition in the U.S. Indeed, two days after NATO's statement, multiple theater chains including AMC Theaters, Regal Theaters, and ArcLight Cinemas announced a reduction in seating capacity by at least 50 percent to address the quickening spread around the country (McNary, "Movie Theaters").

The reductions were only in a place a few days when several states including New York, New Jersey, Ohio, Michigan, Colorado, Washington, and Louisiana ordered the closure of all operating movie theaters (Rubin and Maddaus). In response to the closures, movie studios pulled upcoming films from their schedules as partial releases would not generate enough theatrical revenue to justify distribution and marketing costs. By March 21st, Comscore suspended box office reporting as so few theaters were open in the U.S. and abroad and there were no new films in the theatrical pipeline for the foreseeable future (McNary, "Film News").

The speed at which the U.S. exhibition industry shut down was unimaginable even a few weeks prior. AMC's chief executive officer (CEO) Adam Aron claimed in an earnings report in late February that the mandated closure of about twenty AMC-owned theaters in Italy had not affected the company significantly: "As best as we can tell, the economic impact on AMC from the coronavirus has been minimal. While it's conceivable that could change, as of today, our theaters, which are predominantly in the United States and northern Europe, appear to have felt little or no pain" (qtd. in Vlessing, "AMC Theatres Reports"). Estimates of the losses from the closures of AMC's Italian theaters ranged from $500,000 to $1 million at the time of Aron's statement, a very small amount compared to the company's first quarter revenues (Vlessing, "AMC Theatres Reports"). Less than three weeks later, however, the company announced the closure of all AMC theaters in the U.S. for six to twelve weeks. Operating the largest number of theaters in the U.S. (over 600 locations contributing to nearly 11,000 screens total worldwide), AMC's speedy shift from relative nonchalance to concern was therefore quite remarkable (McClintock, "AMC, Cinemark"). With so many domestic theaters, it was clear that the closures would significantly affect AMC's bottom line in a way that the Italian theater closures had not.

As the pandemic raged across the U.S., numerous news articles and commentaries raised concerns about the viability of movie theaters given the impact of these unprecedented closures. As the shutdowns began in March 2020, an essay by Peter Savodnik for *Vanity Fair* posed the question "Can Movie Theaters Survive Coronavirus?" while Eliana Dockterman of *Time* asked the same thing in reference to the usage of streaming services increasing 13% in just week one of the closures (Savodnik; Dockterman). They were hardly alone in this regard; even six months from the initial closures, Diep Tran of *Backstage* posed the identical question (Tran). Tran's concern stemmed from the fact that the summer months had been brutal for movie theaters. Mandated closures continued in some states such as New Jersey and Michigan through the summer months, while the two biggest theatrical markets in the U.S.—Los Angeles and New York City—also remained closed. According to media scholar Kate Fortmueller, "Although over half of U.S. theaters had opened by the first weekend of September, during the spring and summer there was no time in which all the venues were open" (75). Given the importance of the summer movie season, where approximately 40% of annual box office revenue is typically earned in the months from May through August, movie theaters were indeed in bad shape as a result of the continued closures (Lang and Rubin). In late September, NATO along with other industry groups such as the Director's Guild of America (DGA) and the Motion Picture Association of America (MPAA) penned a letter to Congress asking for bailout funds for the nation's movie theaters since the vast majority of companies had suffered losses of 75% or more during the second quarter of 2020 (McNary, "Movie Business").

In such a tough environment, many theatrical chains thus struggled during the pandemic. For instance, the Alamo Drafthouse chain filed for Chapter 11 bankruptcy in March 2021, while a month later ArcLight Cinemas announced a permanent closure of all the company's theaters as a result of the pandemic's ongoing financial effects on the industry. While the pandemic was an unprecedented event putting pressure on the exhibition industry, it was hardly the only issue companies were facing. According to Fortmueller, "the pandemic simply sped up inevitable changes" that were already negatively affecting the exhibition industry (91). Indeed, media analyst Richard Greenfield argued that prior to the onset of the pandemic in the U.S., 2020 "was going to be the worst year in movie theater history" as a result of declining ticket sales, streaming services' impact on viewing habits, and a weak slate of studio films (qtd. in Dockterman). The pandemic's arrival in the U.S. only exacerbated each of these issues that theaters were already encountering.

And yet, AMC Entertainment Holdings emerged stronger from the pandemic than when they entered it. As the largest theatrical chain globally, AMC certainly faced enormous financial losses as the pandemic raged on, but the company also found opportunities to expand their business, invest in new partnerships, and contest the studios' growing dependence on streaming services. As such, AMC provides an excellent case study of how the pandemic affected the exhibition industry and how large chains negotiated this challenging time. By addressing the complicated environment that pre-dated COVID-19 as well as the conditions that were unique to the pandemic, AMC emerged as the unquestioned leader in the exhibition industry. Indeed, AMC's ability to overcome these challenges provides a blueprint for what it takes to survive in the theatrical business moving forward as the feature film landscape continues to shift in the post-pandemic environment.

CHALLENGES FACED BY THE EXHIBITION
INDUSTRY PRE-COVID

While the coronavirus pandemic provides an easy point of entry to a discussion about the ability of movie theaters to survive in the long-term, the fact is that the exhibition industry was already under serious duress prior to March 2020. Indeed, three years earlier, the cover of industry trade magazine *Variety* featured the title "Scary Movie," and showcased a lone young woman in a theater watching something on an iPad rather than watching the movie screen in front of her. In his cover story article for that issue, "The Reckoning: Why the Movie Business Is in Big Trouble," Brent Lang discussed why the industry had "ample reason to be fearful" (Lang, "The Reckoning"). Exhibitors were encountering several intertwined problems, chief among them the decreasing movie attendance at theaters, the growth of at-home entertainment options, and the shortening exclusivity of the theatrical window. All these factors contributed to a challenging environment for the exhibition sector and were pressing on the fortunes of theaters before the onset of the coronavirus pandemic.

One of the biggest issues facing movie theaters was the clear decline in domestic moviegoing. Though box office revenue generally grew as a result of increasing ticket prices, the decade 2010 until 2020 saw a mostly steady decrease in the amount of North American box office admissions. While there were a few years of increase in that span, most years saw a drop of 3.5% to 4% in admissions ("Theme Report," 41). For the year 2017, the North American box office saw a 24-year low with only 1.24 billion admissions after a dismal summer box office season (Fuster). Admissions rebounded a bit in 2018 (up to 1.3 billion), but 2019 repeated the measly amount of 1.24 billion ("Theme Report," 41). This low annual amount occurred after a plunge of nearly 20% for winter 2019 at the box office, an eight year low, and a summer box office "meltdown" of 7% from the previous year (Vorel; Rubin and Lang). Though many pointed to factors such as poorly received films or audience's "franchise fatigue" as the cause, Universal's domestic distribution head Jim Orr stressed that ups and downs were natural in the exhibition business: "Back in 2017 there were so many stories that going to the movie theater was done . . . A couple weeks later, *It* opened to $123 million. It's a cyclical business. It's always been that way" (qtd. in Rubin and Lang). Certainly, the business will face stronger or weaker years depending upon the availability and popularity of major titles. But the clear trajectory of admissions during the decade pointed to a growing problem for exhibitors, as moviegoers were increasingly staying home during key times for the theatrical sector.

The decreasing admissions issue was coupled with the growing amount of at-home entertainment options consumers have experienced over the last few decades. In her book *Beyond the Multiplex: Cinema, New Technologies, and the Home,* media scholar Barbara Klinger chronicles the growth of home theater systems—usually including large-screen television sets, updated sound systems, and auxiliary devices such as DVD players—which offer compelling reasons to skip theaters and watch films at home instead. According to Klinger,

> [W]hen it first appeared on the market in the mid-1980s, home theater was expensive and largely reserved for the rich. Through the growing affordability and diversifica-

tion of components, home theater has since become widely available to the middle class. By 1997, approximately thirteen million households in the United States were equipped with the multichannel audio-visual systems characteristic of home theater. By 2000, this figure rose to twenty-two million, or more than 20 percent of homes; early 2004 saw home theater's penetration grow to 30 percent (21-22).

Since the publication of the book in 2006, home theater systems have remained an important entertainment feature of U.S. households as screen size and auxiliary options have continued to increase. By 2015, the average screen size of TV sets had grown to 47 inches, a stark increase from the average of 29 inches a few years earlier (Halzack). By 2019, approximately one-third of U.S. homes had internet-connected smart television sets, while nearly half had streaming devices such as Roku offering access to apps and streaming services (Frankel). Due to the increasing number of U.S. homes featuring smart and/or large-screen television sets, consumers certainly had passable alternatives to the movie screen experience.

Coupled with these home theater options, the number of streaming services offering films, television shows, sports, and other live programming has grown significantly as well. Netflix entered the streaming market in 2007 while Hulu launched about a year later, and the range of content available via these services provides new challenges to theaters. These more established services began to release original content towards the beginning of the 2010s in addition to offering their library content, while the end of the decade saw most of the major studios launch their own proprietary services. Studio-backed streaming services such as Disney+ (launched in November 2019) or HBO Max (launched in May 2020) have the infrastructure in place to produce and release a slate of original series without the use of television networks and original films without the need for theaters. According to media scholar Amanda D. Lotz, "Series produced for studio portals are meant for that portal's library; priorities are not split between competing first and second market dynamics;" in other words, all revenue remains with the studio rather than sharing with a network partner (*Portals,* 74). Similarly, original films released through studio-owned streaming services (or portals as Lotz terms them) do not split revenue with exhibitors. Prior to the onset of the pandemic, Disney+ announced a slate of original films exclusive to the service that normally may have been released in theaters including the live action remake of *Lady and the Tramp* (2019), a film based on the true story of heroic sled dog *Togo* (2019), and the remake of *Black Beauty* (2020). The regular release of exclusive originals is necessary to not only keep consumers subscribing on a monthly or annual basis, but also to draw in new subscribers who want to access notable titles. In 2016, U.S. consumers spent $7.8 billion on streaming services; by 2019, that number had doubled and outpaced domestic box office grosses ("Theme Report," 14). With the draw of original series and films, streaming service subscriptions skyrocketed in the decade before the pandemic.

While originals are imperative for the growth and maintenance of subscribers, streaming services (with the exception of Apple TV+) rely on libraries for the majority of their content base. This is where the acquisition of key titles, such as blockbuster films, is central to the subscription business model as they continue to add marquee value to a given service. To take advantage of marketing efficiencies and achieve quicker routes to profitability, the major studios have been steadily shrinking the exclusivity of the theatrical window. In 1997, the average amount of time between theatrical release and the next window release for studio titles was 5 months, 22 days; ten years later, that number had decreased to 4 months, 19 days; by 2017, the number was down to 3 months, 11 days ("Average Video"). A year later, the length was less than 3 months. As the wait time shrinks between windows, consumers have been opting to skip theatrical releases for certain types of films and waiting for them to appear via video-on-demand or streaming services more quickly. For example, during the first six months of 2019, revenue for indie films screened in movie theaters decreased thirty percent from the previous year (Rubin and Lang). Similarly, no original comedy had opened above $20 million in 2019 until *Good Boys* did in August, leaving *New York Times* columnist Brooks Barnes to surmise about the genre's plight: "Moviegoers in North America have given a cold shoulder to one comedy after another in recent months . . . The carnage has prompted speculation that streaming services have made it easy for audiences looking for laughs to skip theaters" (Barnes). Certain types of films were thus seeing significant declines in moviegoers prior to the pandemic, though these same films may have remained popular with audiences via streaming services.

In this environment, AMC began challenging streaming services' pull with consumers, particularly in leading fights with Netflix. In early 2019, the company refused to include Netflix's Academy Award-nominated film *Roma* in its annual Best Picture Showcase, stressing in a statement: "Academy members nominated a film that was never licensed to AMC to play in our theatres. As such, it is not included in the AMC Best Picture Showcase" (McClintock, "Oscars"). AMC was joined by Regal Theaters, the second largest U.S. theatrical chain, and Cinemark, the third largest, in excluding *Roma* from the showcase. Later in 2019, the three chains refused to program Netflix's *The Irishman* after the streamer would not budge on the exhibitors' demands for an exclusive three-month theatrical window (Sims). Asked about how to keep the theatrical experience at the forefront of the streaming era, especially given the popularity of Netflix with consumers, AMC's Executive Vice President of Worldwide Programming Elizabeth Frank stated that "We have to stay compelling. There is a necessity for the theatrical business to continue to evolve and be worthy of consumers' time and their money" (qtd. in McClintock, "AMC Theatres'"). Key in Frank's statement is the idea of offering a "compelling" experience that draws consumers out of their homes and to the movie theaters.

In an attempt to ensure their worthiness for consumers, exhibitors like AMC combatted the growing popularity of streaming and at-home entertainment options by upgrading the theatrical experience for moviegoers. This included an expansion of menu items in many locations, as well as elevating visual, audio, and seating capabilities at theaters. For example, AMC had about ten locations serving alcohol in 2010 and had reached its 300th location doing so in 2018 (Rushing). At the same time, the company was replacing traditional seating with luxury recliners in the majority of its locations. Cinemark's cost to renovate an individual auditorium's seating was approximately $250,000, and AMC's was likely around the same amount (Rushing). As the pandemic gripped the world's theaters, however, these upgrades were for naught: "In the prepandemic world, movie theaters had increasingly focused on ways to enhance the space and experience of theatergoing in ways that were, unfortunately, useless during the pandemic" (Fortmueller, 69). The expensive upgrades to theaters saddled companies like AMC with debt long before the global coronavirus outbreak, and certainly could not help generate revenue for the company when closure mandates were put into effect.

The debt issue was very clear on AMC's bottom line in the year before the pandemic. Attendance at AMC Theaters was down over 12% in the first quarter of 2019, with the company posting a loss of over $130 million in that time frame (Vlessing, "AMC Theatres Swings"). In August, a few dozen corporate employees were laid off as part of an organizational restructure in an attempt to better economize (Bond). By the end of the year, AMC had started to turn some of its fortunes around and ended up outperforming its total 2018 revenues by about $40 million ("AMC Entertainment Holdings"). Despite the domestic box office dropping in overall revenues, AMC had instituted a few changes that helped generate revenue outside of box office ticket sales and created "compelling" reasons to watch movies with AMC. First, the company's movie subscription service, Stubs A-List (which launched in June 2018), reached 900,000 members by November 2019 (Vlessing, "AMC Theatres Loss"). In addition to generating income from its monthly membership fees, the service also encouraged consumers to attend more films and buy more concessions. Second, in October 2019, the company launched an on-demand service with films for sale or rent. AMC's CEO Aron suggested in the press release that this was a natural extension of the theatrical experience: "AMC Theatres is in a unique position to promote specific movies with greater personalization than has ever been possible before . . . . Through the launch of AMC Theatres On Demand, we can reach movie lovers directly and make it easy for them to access films digitally" (qtd. in McNary, "AMC Entertainment"). While it is unclear how much revenue the service generated prior to the pandemic, it did start to expand AMC's reach beyond the theatrical experience. Even with these alternative revenue generators, though, AMC suffered nearly $150 million in losses for 2019, compared to a profit of $110 million the previous year ("AMC Entertainment Holdings"). Thus, months before the coronavirus pandemic reached the U.S., AMC was already in a difficult financial position adapting to the challenges facing the exhibition industry.

NEGOTIATING THE PANDEMIC: AMC AND THE QUEST FOR A "NEW NORMAL"

As local, state, and international mandates went into effect beginning in March 2020, the immediate impact on theaters was on their overall financial infrastructures. Without revenue coming in as a result of the closures, debts began to amass significantly. On March 25th, AMC announced that all of its corporate employees—roughly 600 people—would be furloughed, including CEO Aron (Szalai, "Hollywood's Growing"). By the beginning of April, the company had stopped payment to landlords for many of its locations and within weeks, AMC started to see potential lawsuits. For instance, Palm Springs Mile Associates Ltd. filed suit in Florida for $7.5 million in rent money that AMC had not paid (Albarazi). Analysts such as MKM Partners' Eric Handler believed that "Bankruptcy appears likely" for the chain (and other theatrical chains) as a result of the conditions generated by the pandemic (qtd. in Szalai, "AMC Theatres"). Handler believed that AMC would burn through $155 million of its cash reserves per month through July 2020 in a "no-revenue environment," leaving the company financially vulnerable without theaters open by then (Szalai, "AMC Theatres"). Indeed, near the end of July, AMC announced that its U.S. theaters would remain closed until mid- or late-August, further intensifying the company's financial troubles (Szalai and Vlessing).

With movie theaters closed for so long, as well as most public venues, consumers' use of streaming services increased significantly. Streaming usage in U.S. homes for the week of March 16th through the 22nd doubled the amount from the same period in 2019 and that was before new streaming services such as NBCUniversal's Peacock launched later in 2020 (Porter). For the year 2020, subscriptions to streaming services grew 26% to over 1.1 billion (Faughnder). Digital media accounted for over three-quarters of global home entertainment spending in 2020, which is not surprising given the number of theaters closed worldwide due to pandemic. As a result of the theatrical closures, the major studios experimented with their feature film releases. Rather than re-schedule films for when theaters would be open, several studios opted to release feature films on streaming services either as exclusive content or, in some cases, with additional payment options through these services. For example, Universal chose to release *Trolls World Tour*, which was originally scheduled for theatrical release in April 2020, as a $19.99 digital rental through various services, including Fandango (part of the NBCUniversal corporate family). Argued media scholar Roderik Smits about the studios' use of these services during the pandemic: "[T]his is also a moment in time in which transactional video platforms can demonstrate to Hollywood studios that they can generate economic value for their films ... The current situation offers opportunities for transactional platforms to put pressure on conventional release strategies" (Smits). By bypassing the theatrical window, Universal retained more of the film's online rental income in its first three weeks of availability. At $80 million, this revenue was more than what the studio earned from its share of the total domestic theatrical revenues earned by the film's predecessor, *Trolls,* in 2016 (McClintock, "Theater Owners"). Thus, the film's transactional VOD release strategy considerably benefited the studio.

Theater owners like AMC, however, were not happy with the studios' experimentations with their releases since they cut the exhibitors out completely in terms of revenue. Representing exhibitors' views, trade organization NATO issued a statement following the success of Universal's *Trolls World Tour* stressing that this release strategy "should not be interpreted as a sign of a 'new normal' for Hollywood" (*"Trolls World Tour"*). AMC's CEO Aron responded by banning all Universal films, though that ban would be hard to enforce with all domestic AMC theaters closed and with the studio's major franchises such as *F9* (the ninth film in the *Fast and the Furious* franchise) in the studio's pipeline. Nor was Universal the only studio adopting online release strategies for upcoming feature films. Warner Bros. quickly followed suit with *Scoob!* in April 2020 and Disney with *Mulan* in August 2020, offering the films for premium video rental or purchase options, though Aron did not threaten these two other major studios with any bans. Given the option of generating video-on-demand revenue for feature films, the major studios indeed chose to release several films this way rather than wait for theaters to re-open. Argues Fortmueller about the studios' opportunities during the pandemic to try new release strategies: "[D]uring the pandemic studios were well positioned as compared to hard-hit exhibitors who were merely trying to survive the pandemic closures" (78). With direct pipelines into consumers' homes, the studios had ample opportunities to experiment while exhibitors struggled.

Though Aron was likely unable to maintain a ban against

all Universal films, his stance was notable as the first clash of the pandemic between the studios and the theaters. For the studios, the pandemic was a clear opportunity to try different theatrical release strategies and learn more about feature film's place on their streaming services. Lotz argues in her book *Media Disrupted: Surviving Pirates, Cannibals, and Streaming Wars*:

> The pandemic allowed studios the opportunity to experiment and gather data about direct-to-streaming performance at a variety of price points and with different types of films without fear of retribution from theaters. As the scale of the pandemic varied globally, it also allowed natural experiments as movies that shifted to streaming services ... played in theaters everywhere. The pandemic enabled studios to learn far more about what they stood to lose or gain in negotiating with theater owners for more flexibility over film releases (16).

Particularly of note in Lotz's statement is how these new strategies affected negotiations with theater owners going forward. Representing the largest global theater chain, Aron's statement banning Universal films might not have been enforceable, but it was certainly a warning sign about the studios' experiments with feature film releases and the role of exhibitors in the future. And indeed, AMC was able to achieve concessions from several major studios during the pandemic despite the successes they experienced while experimenting with features films available via transactional video-on-demand and their streaming services.

The first of these concessions occurred in late July 2020, when AMC announced an agreement to reduce the theatrical window exclusivity in their domestic theaters for Universal releases to just 17 days before they could premiere in the next window. As part of that agreement, AMC received a percentage (estimated to be ten percent) of the studio's online rental revenue for properties that originally had a theatrical release. Aron stressed that the agreement was not only good for AMC, but the overall industry as well:

> AMC enthusiastically embraces this new industry model both because we are parti-ci-pating in the entirety of the economics of the new structure, and because premium video on demand creates the added potential for increased movie studio profitability, which should in turn lead to the green-lighting of more theatrical movies. This multi-year agreement preserves exclusivity for theatrical viewing for at least the first three weekends of a film's release, during which time a considerable majority of a movie's theatrical box office revenue typically is generated (qtd. in McClintock, "AMC Theatres, Universal").

According to Aron's statement, the agreement benefitted AMC precisely because the exhibitor could partake in the "entirety of the economics" of Universal's new film releases. The second major concession occurred when AMC struck a similar agreement with Warner Bros. a year later after a contentious period between the two companies. In December 2020, the studio announced that all its films would debut simultaneously in theaters and on its streaming service HBO

Max for the year 2021. At the time of the Warner Bros. announcement, Aron did not ban the studio's films from its theaters but claimed: "As for AMC, we will do all in our power to ensure that Warner does not do so at our expense. We will aggressively pursue economic terms that preserve our business" (qtd. in Galuppo). After multiple Warner Bros. films underperformed at the box office in 2021, the announcement of the 45-day exclusive theatrical window with AMC in August of that year suggested that the major studios did not always benefit from these new release strategies. In response to the announcement, Aron highlighted that these window deals would become more of the norm: "We're especially pleased Warner Bros. has decided to move away from day-and-date . . . We are in active dialogue with every major studio" (qtd. in McClintock, "Warner Bros."). In fact, both Paramount and Disney had already announced exclusive theatrical window releases of 30 to 45 days earlier in 2021, suggesting that the major studios did indeed see a crucial role for exhibitors in the future (Loria & Pahle; Gartenberg). Thus, despite the plentiful opportunities to eschew traditional theatrical releases, the major studios learned through these experiments how important the exhibitors' role remained in the success of many feature films.

Still, with theaters largely closed around the U.S. and abroad as a result of the pandemic, AMC and other exhibitors faced other challenges with their business besides streaming services, particularly in terms of the financial strain. In April 2020, AMC announced that it had raised $500 million in new debt to sustain the company during the theatrical closures (Hayes). This added to the nearly $5 billion in debt that AMC had already obtained prior to the pandemic (Szalai, "Hollywood's Growing"). The acquisition of additional debt helped quell immediate bankruptcy concerns and increased the company's stock price, but it certainly did not point to a company well-positioned financially. In June 2020, the company in a public filing suggested that "substantial doubt exists about our ability to continue as a going concern for a reasonable period of time," highlighting the prolonged financial impact of the pandemic (Bomey, "AMC Theater Chain"). Initial plans to open the majority of its U.S. locations in mid-July were pushed back as a result of the continued mandates in several states as well as the studios' reluctance to release any new films, though about one-third of AMC locations in Europe and the Middle East had reopened by then (Szalai & Vlessing). Even when theaters did open back up at reduced capacities, AMC's fourth quarter results in 2020 were far from stellar with less than 5 million domestic tickets sold (Bomey, "Movie Theater Chain"). Indeed, AMC lost $4.6 billion in 2020 largely as a result of the pandemic's closure of movie theaters globally and was trading just a bit over $2 per share at the end of the year (Lang, "AMC Theatres Lost"). In December 2020, the company stated in an official filing how dire their financial outlook was: "In the absence of additional liquidity, the company anticipates that existing cash resources will be depleted during January 2021" (Szalai, "AMC Theatres Boosts"). Like many exhibitors during the pandemic, AMC significantly struggled as moviegoing remained an impossibility in many markets.

With its financial status so bleak at the end of 2020, the start of 2021 offered a huge turnaround for AMC, however. In January, WallStreetBets, a loosely tied together investment group through Reddit, encouraged investing in AMC stocks by posting a series of memes with the hashtag #SaveAMC. On January 27th, the hashtag trended on Twitter, encouraging new investors who helped the company's stock price jump 300% to over $20, the first time AMC's stock was valued that high since September 2018 (Weprin). AMC's stock was the most traded worldwide that day. The immediate effect of the meme stock purchases was evident; on January 28th, AMC converted $700 million in debt into equity and had a market capitalization of $2.2 billion versus $220 million earlier in the month (Salmon). The meme stock craze was fortunate timing for AMC, as they had just announced a new equity and debt financing deal for over $900 million a few days prior (Szalai, "AMC Theatres Boosts"). Between the new deal and the #SaveAMC campaign, the company's fortunes for 2021 were a vast improvement from a month prior, and AMC's future looked much brighter.

Indeed, with the growing access to the first COVID-19 vaccines and mandates being removed or loosened around the U.S. and the globe in late 2020 and at the start of 2021, AMC's primary business started to see a bit of a rebound. Announced in October 2020, AMC piloted a program to offer private theater rentals in select locations starting at $99, helping boost fourth-quarter earnings. According to a company spokesperson, AMC received 110,000 contacts in just four weeks for theater rentals, a successful launch that encouraged a nation-wide rollout of the program in 2021 (Eggertsen). By the middle of March 2021, 98% of U.S. AMC theaters were open, albeit many in reduced capacities (Chapman). This timing was fortuitous as Warner Bros. released *Godzilla vs. Kong*, its first big blockbuster of the pandemic era, in foreign territories on March 24 and in the U.S. on March 31, providing a huge windfall for AMC. The exhibitor's stock increased 13% based on the film's surprisingly strong opening weekend ticket sales in the U.S. (Epstein). In early June, AMC announced it had received over $200 million from an investment firm to acquire and upgrade new theaters, particularly several from the recently shuttered ArcLight Cinema chain in California (Szalai, "AMC Theatres Raises"). Throughout 2021 and into 2022, the company continued to acquire individual theaters from chains suffering from the effects of the pandemic, in the process strengthening their position in the exhibition market.

Still, the pandemic made it clear that an industry based almost solely on in-person interactions was a liability should future mandates be instituted in the U.S. and around the globe. While AMC grew its primary theatrical business, it also began to invest in new opportunities to expand its revenue potential. One of the more unusual moves by AMC was to purchase a 22% stake of gold and silver mining company Hycroft Mining Holding Corp. Stating that there were a number of financial similarities between the companies, CEO Aron highlighted the added value the diversified asset would bring AMC: "[This is a] truly terrific opportunity to potentially strengthen and enrich our company, and thereby create significant value for AMC Entertainment shareholders . . . It is appealing that the investment requires the commitment of only a nominal amount of AMC cash" (qtd. in Rubin). Requiring more financial investment than this $28 million acquisition was AMC's efforts to launch a retail popcorn brand. Called AMC Theatres Perfectly Popcorn, the venture would introduce fresh popped gourmet popcorn in mall kiosks around the country beginning in 2022, while offering a microwave version in grocery and convenience stores at the end of the year (McClintock, "AMC Theatres Cooks"). A logical expansion of the concession aspect of the exhibition business, the popcorn venture had the potential to generate revenue even if mandated closures affected theaters again in the future.

Another logical expansion of AMC's core business was to increasingly invest fans in the well-being of the company as well as in the key feature films being released in its theaters. In an interview in November 2021, Aron highlighted the need for AMC to expand its focus: "[L]et us think boldly about how we can transform to a new company that does more than just show movies in cinemas" (qtd. in Goldsmith). In the interview, he suggested other possible future expansion opportunities for AMC including film production, a branded credit card, AMC merchandize, and eSports collaborations, none of which have come to fruition thus far, but which highlight new ways for movie fans to engage with the company possibly in the future (Goldsmith). But AMC has made strong efforts in relation to one area of expansion that he noted: NFTs. NFTs (non-fungible tokens) are digital assets typically purchased through internet-based outlets (often via cryptocurrency) and encoded as verified originals of the content. In just the third quarter of 2021, NFTs represented a near $11 billion market so Aron's suggestion of AMC's investment in NFTs was particularly prescient (Locke). AMC has used NFTs in two ways to engage consumers, one targeting movie fans specifically and one targeting new stockholders in the company who invested during or since the meme stock phenomenon.

The company's foray into NFTs began in late November 2021, when AMC and Sony Pictures announced a partnership to offer an exclusive *Spider-Man: No Way Home* NFT to a limited number of fans who purchased advance tickets to the film. Offering approximately 86,000 NFTs to Stubs A-List members and AMC investors, the collaboration was the first time a studio and a theater chain had created such a promotion to help generate ticket sales ("Sony Pictures"). All the exclusive NFTs were snapped up in a matter of hours on November 30th, which became the second highest one-day ticket sale in AMC's history (Aron, "You Were Right").

The compelling interest in the exclusive offer caused multiple movie ticket servers to crash. Based on the success of this first entry into NFTs, AMC announced a few days later an exclusive NFT for the company's 425,000 Investor Connect members ("AMC Theatres and Wax"). The "I Own AMC" NFT rewarded those who had joined the nascent Investor Connect program which was launched in June 2021, and the program's goal was to provide benefits to the stockholders who had invested in AMC since the meme stock phenomenon earlier in the year. Aron emphasized that based on the success of both the Sony promotion and the "I Own AMC" exclusive, "I can say with certainty there will be more NFTs in AMC's future" (qtd. in "AMC Theatres and Wax").

Indeed, as investors were collecting their limited edition NFTs, AMC announced a partnership in February 2022 with Warner Bros. to offer an exclusive *The Batman* NFT similar to its Sony promotion. In his statement about the partnership, Aron emphasized the company's target audience of fans: "Rewarding early ticket purchasers with this limited edition *The Batman* NFT will deliver fans more of the franchise they love" (qtd. in "AMC Theatres Announces"). Demand for the exclusive NFT and tickets helped drive AMC to obtain more than 29% market share of U.S. revenue for *The Batman* in its first weekend in theaters, with eight out of the top 10 ticket selling locations belonging to the AMC chain ("AMC Theatres Enjoys"). AMC's extension into the NFT market thus benefitted their primary business of theatrical ticket sales. In July 2022, the company offered a second exclusive NFT for its Investor Connect members, this time emphasizing their acquisition of Hycroft via a gold mining theme (Aron, "Investor Connect"). That same month, AMC announced an NFT promotion with Sony for the upcoming film *Bullet Train,* their second such collaboration.

The success of these NFT endeavors, along with AMC's expansion into other businesses, its acquisition of theaters, and its fight against streaming services all helped the once endangered company look strong in 2022. Indeed, during the first quarter of 2022, AMC had a box office attendance of 39 million, four times what it saw in the same period of 2021; revenues increased to five times versus the same period in 2021; and food and beverage sales increased eight and a half times from the same period a year earlier as well (Zambonin). The company's second quarter was even better, reaching over 59 million tickets sold as a result of huge hits at the box office such as Paramount's *Top Gun: Maverick* (Lang, "AMC Losses"). In July 2022, box office attendance at AMC Theaters was outpacing July 2019 by 12% (Whitten). As it approached the second half of 2022, AMC was well positioned for an outstanding year having left many of the challenges it faced prior to and during the pandemic behind them.

CONCLUSION: AMC "MAKE[S] MOVIES BETTER"

In the midst of AMC's rebound in late 2021, the company launched an unprecedented marketing campaign to encourage consumers to return to movie theaters in light of the pandemic's lessening impact around the world. AMC spent $25 million to produce the spots and to distribute the campaign to movie theaters and television networks globally (Rubin, "AMC Theatre Shells"). While using Academy Award-level talent including actress Nicole Kidman, cinematographer Jeff Cronenweth, and writer Billy Ray, the spots stressed that AMC Theaters "Make Movies Better" by emphasizing what the moviegoing experience entails emotionally and physically ("AMC Theatres. We Make Movies Better"). According to Aron, the company created the campaign as a result of its success navigating the pandemic and to help re-define to consumers what makes movie theaters an important cultural institution:

> [T]hanks to the billions of dollars we have raised this year, AMC is strong, and it is time for AMC to play on offense again . . . Especially in recent years, AMC and other theatre chains have introduced sophisticated marketing programs to ensure our theatres are relevant. However, relying on 'what's always worked before,' cinema operators have counted on others to undertake significant television advertising campaigns to drive audiences into our buildings . . . With all the change occurring in these uncharted waters in which we now navigate, we believe it is high time for an industry leader like AMC to go on television to remind today's audiences of the magic that can only be found in a movie theatre and at AMC, with our big seats, our big sound and our big screens (qtd. in Rubin, "AMC Theatre Shells").

Aron's statement about the need for the campaign not only addresses the trials the exhibition industry faced during the pandemic, but also the myriad challenges presented to theaters prior to March 2020. By going on the "offense," AMC's campaign stressed what made moviegoing a unique cultural experience and why the company was the perfect conduit for that message on behalf of the exhibition industry.

While the campaign was lampooned and much memed on social media, it circulated right as Hollywood studios began to regularly release bigger films again and audiences seemed to be more comfortable in public spaces as the severity of the pandemic lessened. Indeed, eight of the ten highest grossing films domestically in 2021 were released in the last three months of the year as the campaign continued to play on movie and television screens. In December, *Spider-Man: No Way Home* broke records for the industry and for AMC Theaters, including the largest opening night ever in December and the second highest opening night in the company's history ("AMC Theatres Eclipses"). The first half of 2022 remained strong as new titles like Warner Bros.'s *The Batman* performed well at the box office. The second quarter of 2022 increased over 250% from the same period in 2021 for the entire exhibition industry and represented the strongest quarter since the pandemic began (Williams). While the numbers were not quite at pre-pandemic levels for the entire industry during summer 2022, the box office indicated consumers' strong interest in returning to theaters, despite worries at the start of the pandemic that the business would not survive COVID-19.

And yet, there do remain significant challenges for the exhibition industry in the post-pandemic environment. It is difficult at this time to determine if the increase in box office attendance seen in late 2021/early 2022 is a short blip as people return to more public activities after the pandemic or a longer-term commitment to the theatrical experience. Several chains and individual theaters permanently closed during the pandemic like ArcLight while some have continued to struggle as not all film locations, or all types of films have seen the same rebounds. For example, second run theaters have increasingly had to pivot from their business model as the theatrical window gets shorter for major studio releases while smaller chains like Laemmle Theaters that are focused on art cinema have had to sell off locations to remain afloat

(Gajewski). In addition, the exhibition industry as a whole also faces new challenges in the post-Paramount Decree environment. In August 2020, a federal judge granted the Justice Department's motion to dissolve the decades-long rule keeping studios from owning theater chains. This 1948 Paramount Decree decision was made as a result of the monopolization of the industry that occurred during the Classical Hollywood era. Arguing that today's film landscape is significantly different than the classical studio era, Judge Analisa Torres claimed in her decision: "Given this changing marketplace, the Court finds that it is unlikely that the remaining Defendants would collude to once again limit their film distribution to a select group of theaters in the absence of the Decrees and, finds, therefore, that termination is in the public interest" (qtd. in Gardner). Writers for *Deadline* called the decision "a symbolic thumb in the eye" for exhibitors after enduring the early part of the pandemic (Goldsmith and D'Alessandro). With the possibility that new media companies such as Amazon Prime Video or Netflix in addition to the major studios may purchase theatrical chains, there are concerns about what films will be offered and to what outlets in the future, especially as these companies continue to focus on growing their own streaming services.

Despite any fears of more consolidation in the film exhibition industry, AMC Theaters is in a different position now than when they started in the pandemic. For the time being, movie attendance is on an upswing; the company has lessened the impact of streaming through new partnerships with studios such as Warner Media and Universal; and they have expanded their business, both in terms of the number of theaters they have, and also in reaching new areas such as retail and NFTs. By diversifying its business beyond the theatrical experience, AMC has positioned itself well for the changes that lay ahead in the exhibition industry. As the largest global theatrical chain, they have thus set a standard for others in the industry to follow. While additional challenges will arise affecting the exhibition industry in the post-pandemic world, AMC has established a new normal in the theatrical landscape.

WORKS CITED

Albarazi, Hannah. "AMC Theatres Sued for $7.5M in Unpaid Rent Amid COVID-19." *Law 360* 22 Apr. 2020, https://www.law360.com/articles/1266516/amc-theaters-sued-for-7-5m-in-unpaid-rent-amid-covid-19.

"AMC Entertainment Holdings, Inc. Announces Fourth Quarter and Full Year 2019 Results." *Business Wire* 27 Feb. 2020, https://www.businesswire.com/news/home/20200227005974/en/AMC-Entertainment-Holdings-Inc.-Announces-Fourth-Quarter-and-Full-Year-2019-Results.

"AMC Theatres and Wax to Issue New Exclusive 'I Own AMC' NFT to All Existing and New Members of AMC Investor Connect." *Business Wire* 6 Dec. 2021, https://www.businesswire.com/news/home/20211206005258/en/.

"AMC Theatres Announces Special *The Batman* NFT Promotion for Fans." *Box Office* 8 Feb. 2022, https://www.boxofficepro.com/the-batman-nft-amc-theatres/.

"AMC Theatres Eclipses Box Office Records with *Spider-Man: No Way Home* Achieving Highest December Opening Night Ever, and Second Highest Opening Night of All Time." *AMC Theaters* 17 Dec. 2021, https://investor.amctheatres.com/newsroom/news-details/2021/AMC-Theatres-Eclipses-Box-Office-Records-With-

SPIDER-MAN-NO-WAY-HOME-Achieving-Highest-December-Opening-Night-Ever-and-Second-Highest-Opening-Night-of-All-Time-/default.aspx.

"AMC Theatres Enjoys Its Third-Highest Attended Weekend in Two Years with More Than 4 Million Tickets Sold Globally From Thursday Through Sunday, Based on the Strength of the Successful Opening Weekend of Warner Bros.' THE BATMAN." *Yahoo! Finance* 7 Mar. 2022, https://finance.yahoo.com/news/amc-theatres-enjoys-third-highest-200700166.html.

"AMC Theatres. We Make Movies Better." *YouTube*, uploaded by AMC Theatres, 8 Sept. 2021, https://www.youtube.com/watch?v=KiEeIxZJ9x0.

Aron, Adam [@CEOAdam]. "We honor our 728,00[0] existing members of AMC Investor Connect and new members joining by 9/30/22. You can claim (in October) a free golden NFT from us, and we'll pay your WAX NFT wallet fees for a year. Celebrating our Hycroft Mining investment: "There is Gold in Them Thar Hills." *Twitter*, 8 July 2022, 6:18 AM, https://twitter.com/CEOAdam/status/1545366831510294530.

——. "You were right when so many of you suggested movie themed NFTs. Our Spider-Man NFT is a key reason why No Way Home generated the second highest one day ticket sales in AMC's entire history! All 86,000 NFT's (at one per qualifying member) were fully committed by Monday afternoon." *Twitter*, 30 Nov. 2021, 6:44 PM, https://twitter.com/CEOAdam/status/1465844309492703236.

"Average Video Announcement and Video Release Windows." *National Association of Theatre Owners* 28 Aug.

2019, https://www.natoonline.org/wp-content/uploads /2019/09/Major-Studio-Release-Window-Averages-8_ 28_19.pdf.

Barnes, Brooks. "'Good Boys' Ends Hollywood's Comedy Drought." *New York Times* 19 Aug. 2019, https://www. nytimes.com/2019/08/18/movies/good-boys-box-of-fice-comedy.html.

Bomey, Nathan. "AMC Theater Chain Warns That It May Not Survive Disruption from Coronavirus Pandemic." *USA Today* 3 June 2020, https://www.usatoday.com/ story/money/2020/06/03/amc-theater-coronavirus-covid-19-going-concern/3136597001/.

———. "Movie Theater Chain AMC: 'We Have Reason to Be Optimistic' Despite $4.6 Billion Pandemic Loss." *USA Today* 10 Mar. 2021, https://www.usatoday.com/story/ money/2021/03/10/amc-movies-covid-pandemic-earnings/6946381002/.

Bond, Paul. "AMC Theatres Lays Off 35 Corporate Staffers Amid Restructuring." *The Hollywood Reporter* 22 Aug. 2019, https://www.hollywoodreporter.com/movies/mo vie-news/amc-theatres-lays-35-corporate-staffers-restr ucturing-1233892/.

Chapman, Michelle. "Prepare the Popcorn: AMC Open-ing More Movie Theaters." *ABC News* 18 Mar. 2021, https://abcnews.go.com/Entertainment/wireStory/pre pare-popcorn-amc-opening-movie-theaters-76532959.

Dockterman, Eliana. "Streaming Was Already Up 13% Last Weekend. Can Movie Theaters Survive COVID-19?" *Time* 19 Mar. 2020, https://time.com/5806060/corona

virus-movie-theaters-streaming/.

Donnelly, Matt. "CinemaCon 2020 Cancelled over Corona-virus Concerns." *Variety* 11 Mar. 2020, https://variety.com/2020/film/news/cinemacon-2020-cancelled-coronavirus-1203529527/.

Eggertsen, Chris. "AMC Announces Availability of Private Theater Rentals at U.S. Locations after Successful Beta Launch." *Box Office* 10 Nov. 2020, https://www.boxofficepro.com/amc-private-theater-rentals-coronavirus/.

Epstein, Adam. "AMC Theatres Got a Lifeline from 'Godzilla vs. Kong.'" *Quartz* 6 Apr. 2021, https://qz.com/1992839/amc-theatres-got-a-lifeline-from-godzilla-vs-kong/.

Faughnder, Ryan. "Streaming Milestone: Global Subscriptions Passed 1 Billion Last Year." *Los Angeles Times* 18 Mar. 2021, https://www.latimes.com/entertainment-arts/business/story/2021-03-18/streaming-milestone-global-subscriptions-passed-1-billion-last-year-mpa-theme-report.

Fortmueller, Kate. *Hollywood Shutdown: Production, Distribution, and Exhibition in the Time of COVID.* University of Texas Press, 2021.

Frankel, Daniel. "Smart TV Penetration in U.S. Now up to 32%." *Multichannel News* 31 May 2019, https://www.nexttv.com/news/32-percent-of-us-tvs-are-smart-tvs.

Fuster, Jeremy. "Movie Theater Attendance Hits 24-Year Low; Ticket Prices Rise Nearly 4 Percent." *The Wrap* 17 Jan. 2018, https://www.thewrap.com/movie-theater-attendance-hits-24-year-low-ticket-prices-rise-nearly-4-percent/.

Gajewski, Ryan. "Indie Movie Theater Chains Struggle to Survive as Windows Shorten." *The Hollywood Reporter* 10 Mar. 2022, https://www.hollywoodreporter.com/business/business-news/indie-movie-theater-chains-struggle-to-survive-as-windows-shorten-1235107040/.

Galuppo, Mia. "AMC Theatres Says Warner Bros.' Streaming Plan Will 'Sacrifice' Studio Profits." *The Hollywood Reporter* 3 Dec. 2020, https://www.hollywoodreporter.com/movies/movie-news/amc-theatres-says-warner-bros-streaming-plan-will-sacrifice-studio-profits-4100058/.

Gardner, Eriq. "Judge Agrees to End Paramount Consent Decrees." *The Hollywood Reporter* 7 Aug. 2020, https://www.hollywoodreporter.com/business/business-news/judge-agrees-end-paramount-consent-decrees-1306387/.

Gartenberg, Chaim. "Disney's Return to Theaters Will Include a Shorter 45-Day Theatrical Window." *The Verge* 13 May 2021, https://www.theverge.com/2021/5/13/22434964/disney-theatrical-window-45-days-shorter-streaming-shang-chi-free-guy.

Goldsmith, Jill. "AMC Entertainment's Reddit Investors Want It to Make Movies (Again), a Branded Credit Card, AMC Cryptocurrency—Could Be, Says CEO Adam Aron." *Deadline* 8 Nov. 2021, https://deadline.com/2021/11/amc-entertainment-ceo-adam-aron-box-office-movie-theaters-1234870146/.

Goldsmith, Jill, and Anthony D'Alessandro. "With Exhibition on the Brink, Paramount Decree Topples, a Symbolic Thumb in the Eye." *Deadline* 7 Aug. 2020, https://deadline.com/2020/08/paramount-consent-decrees-exhibition-shutdown-coronavirus-windows-universal-amc-1203007920/.

Halzack, Sarah. "The Rise of the Really-Big-Screen TV." *The Washington Post* 24 Nov. 2015, https://www.washington-post.com/news/business/wp/2015/11/24/the-rise-of-the-really-big-screen-tv/.

Hayes, Dade. "AMC Issues $500M in Debt to Stay Liquid; Shares Spike on U.S. Reopening Plan." *Deadline* 17 Apr. 2020, https://deadline.com/2020/04/amc-issues-500m-in-debt-to-stay-liquid-shares-spike-on-u-s-reopening-plan-1202910780/.

Klinger, Barbara. *Beyond the Multiplex: Cinema, New Technologies, and the Home.* University of California Press, 2006.

Lang, Brent. "AMC Losses Narrow, Theater Chain Rewards Retail Investors with 'Ape' Dividend." *Variety* 4 Aug. 2022. https://variety.com/2022/film/news/amc-earnings-ape-dividend-1235333828/.

———. "AMC Theatres Lost $4.6 Billion in 2020 Due to COVID-19." *Variety* 10 Mar. 2021. https://variety.com/2021/film/news/amc-theatres-4-6-billion-loss-covid-1234927642/.

———. "The Reckoning: Why the Movie Business Is in Big Trouble." *Variety* 27 Mar. 2017, https://variety.com/2017/film/features/movie-business-changing-consumer-demand-studios-exhibitors-1202016699/.

Lang, Brent, and Rebecca Rubin. "Will the Coronavirus Pandemic Wipe Out All of Summer Blockbuster Season?" *The Hollywood Reporter* 31 Mar. 2020, https://variety.com/2020/film/news/summer-movies-fast-9-coronavirus-ghostbusters-afterlife-wonder-woman-1984-1203550310/.

Locke, Taylor. "NFT Trading Volume Hit $10.7 Billion Last Quarter—Here Are 2 Reasons Why People Are Spending Thousands on Digital Assets." *CNBC* 6 Oct. 2021, https://www.cnbc.com/2021/10/06/nft-trading-volume-hit-10-billion-2-reasons-why-people-are-buying.html.

Loria, Daniel, and Rebecca Pahle. "Paramount Cuts Down Theatrical Exclusivity for Major Titles to 30-45 Day Window." *Box Office* 24 Feb. 2021, https://www.boxofficepro.com/paramount-cuts-down-theatrical-exclusivity-for-major-titles-to-30-45-day-window/.

Lotz, Amanda D. *Media Disrupted: Surviving Pirates, Cannibals, and Streaming Wars.* MIT Press, 2021.

——. *Portals: A Treatise on Internet-Distributed Television.* Michigan Publishing, 2017.

McClintock, Pamela. "AMC, Cinemark Close All U.S. Theaters as Cinemas across the Country Go Dark amid Coronavirus." *The Hollywood Reporter* 16 Mar. 2020, https://www.hollywoodreporter.com/movies/movie-news/amc-theatres-close-all-locations-as-cinemas-us-go-dark-1285012/.

——. "AMC Theatres Cooks Up Retail Popcorn Business." *The Hollywood Reporter* 4 Nov. 2021, https://www.hollywoodreporter.com/business/business-news/amc-theatres-diversifying-retail-popcorn-business-1235042564/.

——. "AMC Theatres' Elizabeth Frank Talks 'The Irishman' and the Netflix Debate." *The Hollywood Reporter* 15 Oct. 2019, https://www.hollywoodreporter.com/movies/movie-news/elizabeth-frank-talks-joker-release-irishman-netflix-debate-1245606/.

———. "AMC Theatres, Universal Collapsing Theatrical Window to 17 Days in Unprecedented Pact." *The Hollywood Reporter* 28 July 2020, https://www.hollywoodreporter.com/movies/movie-news/amc-theatres-universal-colla psing-theatrical-window-17-days-unprecedented-pa ct-1304759/.

———. "Oscars: Major Theater Chains Bar Netflix's 'Roma' from Best Picture Showcase." *The Hollywood Reporter* 22 Jan. 2019, https://www.hollywoodreporter.com/movies /movie-news/amc-regal-cinemark-bar-netflixs-roma-best-picture-showcase-1177952/.

———. "Theater Owners Decry Universal's 'Trolls World Tour' On-Demand Significance." *The Hollywood Reporter* 28 Apr. 2020, https://www.hollywoodreporter.com/news /general-news/theater-owners-decry-universals-tr olls-world-tour-demand-performance-1292242/.

———. "Warner Bros., AMC Strike 45-Day Exclusive Theatrical Window Deal for 2022." *The Hollywood Reporter* 9 Aug. 2021, https://www.hollywoodreporter.com/mov ies/movie-news/warner-bros-commits-to-exclusive-theatrical-release-in-2022-in new-amc-theatre-deal-1234995035/.

McNary, Dave. "AMC Entertainment Introducing On-Demand Movie Service." *Variety* 14 Oct. 2019, https:// variety.com/2019/film/news/amc-entertainment-mov ies-on-demand-1203370464/.

———. "Film News Roundup: Weekend Box Office Reporting Suspended Due to Coronavirus." *Variety* 20 Mar. 2020, https://variety.com/2020/film/news/weekend-box-of fice-reporting-suspended-coronavirus-1203541099/.

———. "Movie Business Leaders Urge Congress to Fund Theater Bailout." *Variety* 30 Sep. 2020, https://variety.com/2020/film/news/movie-theaters-congress-bailout-1234788302/.

———. "Movie Theaters Cut Seating Capacity over Coronavirus." *Variety* 13 Mar. 2020, https://variety.com/2020/film/news/movie-theater-chains-limiting-salescoronavirus-1203534095/.

Porter, Rick. "Streaming Gets Big Bump During Coronavirus Quarantines, Nielsen Says." *The Hollywood Reporter* 31 Mar. 2020, https://www.hollywoodreporter.com/tv/tv-news/streaming-gets-big-bump-coronavirus-quarantines-nielsen-says-1287682/.

Rubin, Rebecca. "AMC Theatre Shells Out $25 Million for Ad Campaign to Get People Back to the Movies." *Variety* 8 Sept. 2021, https://variety.com/2021/film/news/amc-campaign-back-to-the-movies-1235058227/.

———. "AMC Theatres Buys $28 Million Stake in Gold and Silver Mining Company." *Variety* 15 Mar. 2022, https://variety.com/2022/film/news/amc-theatres-stake-gold-silver-mining-company-1235205937/.

Rubin, Rebecca, and Brent Lang. "Summer Box Office Meltdown: Why the Movie Business Is Running Scared." *Variety* 2 July 2019, https://variety.com/2019/film/news/summer-box-office-movie-business-downturn-1203256608/.

Rubin, Rebecca, and Gene Maddaus. "Movie Theaters in These States Are Closed Due to Coronavirus." *Variety* 16 Mar. 2020, https://variety.com/2020/film/news/movie-theaters-close-u-s-coronavirus-1203536126/.

Rushing, Ellie. "AMC, Cinemark Up Their Game with Enhanced Seating, Dining Options." *South Florida Sun Sentinel* 23 July 2018, https://www.sun-sentinel.com/business/fl-reg-movie-theaters-renovations-income-20180716-story.html.

Salmon, Felix. "Reddit Traders' Real-World Positive Consequences." *Axios* 28 Jan. 2021, https://www.axios.com/2021/01/28/reddit-gamestop-amc-stocks-debt.

Savodnik, Peter. "Can Movie Theaters Survive Coronavirus Crisis?" *Vanity Fair* 19 Mar. 2020, https://www.vanityfair.com/hollywood/2020/03/can-movie-theaters-survive-coronavirus.

Sims, David. "Why Big Movie Chains Won't Show Martin Scorsese's Netflix Epic." *The Atlantic* 28 Aug. 2019, https://www.theatlantic.com/entertainment/archive/2019/08/netflixs-irishman-wont-be-shown-major-theaters-martin-scorsese/596989/.

Smits, Roderik. "How Hollywood Studios and Online Video Platforms are Responding." *Flow* 21 Apr. 2020, https://www.flowjournal.org/2020/04/coronavirus-online-video-platforms-respond/.

"Sony Pictures and AMC Theatres Choose WAX Blockchain for *Spider-Man: No Way Home* NFT Promotion." *Business Wire* 30 Nov. 2021, https://www.businesswire.com/news/home/20211130005920/en/Sony-Pictures-and-AMC-Theatres-Choose-WAX-Blockchain-for-Spider-Man-No-Way-Home-NFT-Promotion.

Szalai, Georg. "AMC Theatres 'Bankruptcy Appears Likely,' Analyst Says." *The Hollywood Reporter* 9 Apr. 2020, https:

//www.hollywoodreporter.com/movies/movie-news
/amc-theatres-bankruptcy-appears-analyst-says-128
9514/.

———. "AMC Theatres Boosts Liquidity, Saying It Has 'Financial Runway Deep into 2021.'" *The Hollywood Reporter* 25
Jan. 2021. https://www.hollywoodreporter.com/busin
ess/business-news/amc-theatres-boosts-liquidity-say
ing-it-has-financial-runway-deep-into-2021-4112973/.

———. "AMC Theatres Raises $230.5M for Acquisitions, In-
vestments via Stock Sale." *The Hollywood Reporter* 1 June
2021, https://www.hollywoodreporter.com/business/b
usiness-news/amc-theatres-raises-million-acquisitions-
investments-1234961260/.

———. "Hollywood's Growing Debt and Earnings Risk amid
the Pandemic: 'It's All About Liquidity.'" *The Hollywood
Reporter* 26 Mar. 2020, https://www.hollywoodreporter.
com/movies/movie-news/hollywoods-debt-grows-risk
ier-pandemic-1286655/.

Szalai, Georg and Etan Vlessing. "AMC Theatres Delays
U.S. Reopening to August." *The Hollywood Reporter* 23
July 2020, https://www.hollywoodreporter.com/movies
/movie-news/amc-theatres-delays-us-reopening-august-
1304083/.

"Theme Report 2020." *Motion Picture Association, Inc.* 18
Mar. 2021, https://www.motionpictures.org/research-d
ocs/2020-theme-report/.

Tran, Diep. "Can Movie Theaters Survive the COVID-19
Pandemic?" *Backstage* 24 Nov. 2020, https://www.back
stage.com/magazine/article/can-movie-theaters-sur
vive-the-covid-19-pandemic-72123/.

"*Trolls World Tour* VOD Revenues Do Not Indicate a Shift in Consumer Movie Viewing Preferences." *National Association of Theatre Owners* 28 Apr. 2020, https://www.natoonline.org/wp-content/uploads/2020/04/TROLLS-WORLD-TOUR-VOD-REVENUES-DO-NOT-INDICATE-SHIFT-IN-CONSUMER-MOVIE-VIEWING-PREFERENCES.pdf.

Vlessing, Etan. "AMC Theatres Loss Narrows on Record Attendance, Stubs A-List Reaches 900,000 Subs." *The Hollywood Reporter* 7 Nov. 2019, https://www.hollywoodreporter.com/business/business-news/amc-theatres-quarterly-loss-narrows-record-attendance-1253080/.

———. "AMC Theatres Reports 'Minimal' Economic Impact from Coronavirus Crisis." *The Hollywood Reporter* 27 Feb. 2020, https://www.hollywoodreporter.com/movies/movie-news/amc-theatres-posts-quarterly-loss-as-attendance-falls-1281635/.

———. "AMC Theatres Swings to a Quarterly Loss, Cites 'Industry-Wide Softness.'" *The Hollywood Reporter* 9 May 2019, https://www.hollywoodreporter.com/movies/movie-news/amc-theatres-swings-quarterly-loss-cites-industry-wide-softness-1209099/.

Vorel, Jim. "Winter 2019 Box Office Numbers Have Hit an 8-Year Low." *Paste Magazine* 18 Feb. 2019, https://www.pastemagazine.com/movies/box-office/winter-2019-box-office-numbers-have-hit-an-8-year/.

Weprin, Alex. "AMC Entertainment Stock Surges, Fueled by Traders on Reddit." *The Hollywood Reporter*, 27 Jan. 2021, https://www.hollywoodreporter.com/business/business-news/amc-entertainment-stock-surges-fueled-by-traders-on-reddit-4122607/.

Whitten, Sarah. "Moviegoers Are Leaving Their Couches for Theaters, Bringing Summer Box Office Sales Close to Pre-Pandemic Levels." *CNBC* 11 July 2022, https://www.cnbc.com/2022/07/11/moviegoers-are-leaving-their-couches-for-theaters-bringing-summer-box-office-sales-close-to-pre-pandemic-levels.html.

Williams, Joseph. "Moviegoers Flock Back to Blockbusters as Summer Box Office Booms." *S&P Global* 13 July 2022, https://www.spglobal.com/marketintelligence/en/news-insights/latest-news-headlines/moviegoers-flock-back-to-blockbusters-as-summer-box-office-booms-8211-s-p-podcast-71126879.

Zambonin, Bernard. "This Could Be a Bad Time to Bet Against AMC. Here's Why." *The Street* 15 June 2022, https://www.thestreet.com/memestocks/amc/this-could-be-a-bad-time-to-bet-against-amc-heres-why.

No Time to Die—Literally: Risk, Fandom, and Theatergoing during the COVID-19 Pandemic

By Tyler Johnson and Lisa Funnell

ABSTRACT

COVID-19 impacted moviegoing and fandom in profound ways. Such concerns were especially acute for properties delayed by the pandemic, like the 25th James Bond film, *No Time to Die*. Original survey research shows that willingness to see the film opening weekend without social distancing was significantly lower amongst Bond fans who still perceived COVID to be a crisis. Interest in returning to the theater in general was also impacted by such assessments of the pandemic.

Keywords: risk, fandom, COVID-19, James Bond

Sin tiempo para morir, literalmente: Riesgo, fanatismo y teatro durante la pandemia de COVID-19

RESUMEN

El COVID-19 afectó profundamente el cinéfilo y el fanatismo. Tales preocupaciones fueron especialmente agudas para las propiedades retrasadas por la pandemia, como la película número 25 de James Bond, *No Time to Die*. La investigación original de la encuesta muestra que la disposición a ver la película el fin de semana de estreno sin distanciamiento social fue significativamente menor entre los fanáticos de Bond que todavía percibían que COVID era una crisis. El interés en volver al teatro en general también se vio afectado por tales evaluaciones de la pandemia.

Palabras clave: riesgo, fanatismo, COVID-19, James Bond

无暇赴死，真的：
2019冠状病毒病大流行期间的风险、
影迷和看电影

摘要：2019冠状病毒病（COVID-19）对电影观看和影迷造成了严重影响。对于因大流行而推迟放映的电影，例如第25部詹姆斯·邦德电影《无暇赴死》，这种担忧尤为严重。原始调查研究表明，对那些仍然认为COVID是一场危机的邦德粉丝而言，在不保持社交距离的情况下观看首映周末电影的意愿显著更低。对大流行的这类评估也影响了重返剧院的兴趣。

关键词：风险，影迷，2019冠状病毒病，詹姆斯·邦德

The economic impact of the COVID-19 global pandemic has been and continues to be far-reaching. One of the sectors hardest hit during this crisis has been entertainment, an industry in which producers of film, television, music, stage, and sporting content had to gauge how best to adapt their work in response to an evolving marketplace in which positive cases, hospitalizations, and deaths ebbed and flowed while the public's willingness to risk leaving their homes and commune with others was ever-changing. At some points, this meant rethinking how content could be created and delivered to cater to a society that, as a by-product of taking the pandemic seriously and following governmental guidelines (for the most part), was seemingly more content to stream popular culture through personal devices than ever before. At others, it meant pressing pause on production and release until a point at which societal situations reached normalcy (or whatever that meant in a COVID-impacted world). As a result, at many moments across 2020 and 2021, the public had to wait longer than expected for sporting teams to resume play, musicians to retake the stage, and film franchises to hit the screen.

No Time to Die, the 25th James Bond film from Eon Productions, is one such example of content whose path to the market was altered by COVID. Originally scheduled for release in April 2020, *No Time to Die*'s debut was delayed on multiple occasions as the pandemic progressed, first to November 2020, then April 2021, and finally October 2021 when it premiered in the United States. As the moviegoing public (and Bond fans specifically in this instance) were forced to be patient, one might wonder how the presence of COVID affected their eagerness to return to the theater for major cinematic events in what we might consider traditional fashion: opening weekend without precautions. Such a question fits into the broader debate over whether assessments of risk shaped how public the public was willing to be in social spaces (not only to consume movies, concerts, theater, and live sports, but also beyond entertainment) at different stages of the global pandemic.

Public opinion research can offer greater insight into the dynamics underlying behaviors related to risk, fandom, and theatergoing during the COVID pandemic. In May 2021, an original survey was conducted that asked respondents to discuss their past and future moviegoing habits, their assessments of the state of COVID-19 at the time, their fandom of the Bond franchise, and their interest in seeing *No Time to Die* in theaters (and under what conditions) upon its release. Results show that while fandom predicted interest in seeing the film in the traditional fashion one might expect for fans (opening weekend without precautions in place), willingness to do so without the implementation of social distancing policies was significantly lower amongst those fans who still perceived COVID to be a crisis. Additionally, this perception of crisis drove the belief that one was less likely to return to the theater in general in the near future if such COVID-related restrictions were not in effect. These findings have clear implications for the relationship between risk, fandom, and participation in society and popular culture phenomena during tumultuous times.

CONSUMERS, RISK, AND THE COVID-19 PANDEMIC

Across all forms of commerce and all points in time, actions taken by consumers, be those actions seemingly mundane or obviously momentous, involve some sort of risk. Individuals have choices to make in the marketplace, and they want to make the right ones. However, they often approach these choices fearing that the decision they make could subsequently prove to be problematic (Taylor 55). As Bauer described in his seminal 1960 work "Consumer Behavior as Risk Taking," uncertain consequences await the consumer faced with a decision, and some of those consequences could be unpleasant (14). However, not every person approaches making decisions in the same way. Some are more self-confident than others, some are more anxious than others, and as a result some are more prone to feeling discomfort with staring down choices than others (Taylor 56).

Scholars depict these differences in how we assess dilemmas as consumers in terms of what has come to be called risk aversion. One individual may respond to a specific risk in completely different ways than another, even if the risk is the same for both (Outreville 159). It is also quite possible that the aforementioned self-confidence or anxiety or discomfort could vary based on the nuances of the decision just as much as they do the person making it. With outcomes only knowable in the future, consumers unsurprisingly search for ways to reduce their risk or delay making choices (Taylor 54). They might attempt to become as educated as they can on the decision at hand. They might try, as best as possible, to assess future positives and negatives, the gains and losses that could result from one option or another, before coming to a final conclusion. They also might wait until conditions become clearer before making a choice or decide that not making a choice is a more satisfying outcome than potentially making the wrong one.

This decision-making calculus might also be affected by a myriad of other factors, some of which are beyond the consumer's control. As Sheth describes, a consumer's social context (e.g., marriage, children, moving), evolving technology, and locally specific rules and regulations can shape behavior (280). A fourth influence on perceptions of risk is the onset of disaster (Cameron and Shah 484; Sheth 280). The COVID-19 global pandemic undoubtedly qualifies as a disaster, and its effects since early 2020 on individual, group, and corporate behavior across multiple spaces, consumer and otherwise, cannot be denied. In terms of consumerism, COVID immediately and lastingly altered what decisions were even available to the public: what one could buy (be that products on a shelf or experiences that entertain), when and where one could buy it, and what it might cost in terms of money or peace of mind. It also forced many to think about risk aversion through a new lens, determining if this brand new, unknown, and constantly evolving threat was enough to force one to rethink their way of life, or if previous processes and patterns on how to live would hold firm.

One type of reaction that made itself clear in the first year of the COVID-19 pandemic was individual cooperation or compliance with measures intended to prevent the spread of the virus. Such reactions were not uniform throughout the public though (Keinan et al. 21). Some members of the public readily followed guidelines handed down by government officials, while others hesitated or even revolted. Research quickly chronicled which types of people opted for which path. Perceptions of the current and upcoming state of the pandemic predicted willingness to follow restrictions (Briscese et al.). Those in the public fearing the worst were suddenly on board with many preventative measures, but others who did not feel this emotion resisted (Harper et al. 1875). Similar dynamics can be seen when it comes to an individual's level of anxiety regarding COVID (Solomou and Constantinidou 1). Negativity and the extent to which someone felt a sense of duty also separated the compliant from the noncompliant (Zajenkowski et al.), as did demographic predictors like gender (Griffith et al. 3). These findings in the specific arena of COVID across 2020 and 2021 paralleled the broader findings on risk aversion that scholars had been quantifying for generations. Various aspects of an individual's personality type mattered. So too did the informational environment in which an individual existed, as that environment shaped how an individual assessed past, present, and future conditions, regardless of accuracy. The challenge of the pandemic may have been new, but many of the broader patterns regarding risk aversion remained valid.

In addition to impacting public behavior, COVID also reshaped the bottom line for countless industries, one of which was entertainment. Estimates one year into the pandemic had COVID-related costs to the bottom line in the tens of billions, as both demand and supply had to be recalculated amidst a changing society (Adgate). Entertainment businesses whose product depended on physical locations and synchronous presentation of content were hardest hit, while those with the flexibility to provide services online benefitted (Ryu and Cho 592). Given these parameters, it is no surprise that venues like movie theaters and concert halls struggled greatly as demand dissipated almost immediately and struggled to return (Ryu and Cho 592); producers of content, cognizant of this slow and shifting demand, had to simultaneously anticipate when COVID would subside and when individuals would be willing to return to congregating together. Estimating either of these, let alone both, proved to be an almost impossible proposition. As a result, the return of many forms of entertainment across the first year or two of the pandemic could best be described as fluid. With great regularity, the return of events like individual concert tours and film premieres were announced and then delayed, be that to a specific future date or indefinitely. At times, entertainment returned after delays, but in a slightly different form than originally planned; for example, many soccer leagues across the globe returned to play after a few months of a COVID-related break but did so in front of empty stadiums. In some circumstances, sponsors of annual events (such as the Wimbledon tennis tournament or golf's The Open Championship) chose to cancel and return a year later rather than deal with the constant uncertainty inherent to the pandemic.

The presence of COVID, however, did not necessarily entail that consumer behavior would be forever changed. According to Pantano et al., risk assessments during the pandemic are not guaranteed to shape how individuals act once the world fully reopens; in their study, consumers expressed a willingness to act how they did before COVID, especially when said opportunities involve some sort of escapism (65). Similarly, consumers can be expected to return to social situations where an in-person experience had value over variations in a digital space prior to the onset of the pandemic (Ryu and Cho 594). One group of individuals who might be expected to pursue escapism as well as value an in-person experience similar to the one they had pre-COVID over a digital one is fans.

FANDOM AMIDST A PANDEMIC AND ITS IMPLICATIONS FOR BOND

Fans are not necessarily just followers or individuals who express interest (Moorhouse 17-23; Tulloch and Jenkins 23). As Linden and Linden add, "fans are consumers" (38). The COVID-19 pandemic put fans in a position to consume in ways that did not resemble what they were used to in the past, closing in-person opportunities for the most part and pushing them into online spaces to try and satisfy their desire for content. Given a lack of options, such isolation could have created ideal conditions for this fandom to intensify further (Andrews 902). At the same time, brands producing content had to consider whether they could recreate or maintain the sense of community and belonging they had fostered amongst fans in the weeks, months, and years before COVID spread (Mastromartino et al. 1711). Such efforts were especially complicated in fan spaces where highly anticipated content scheduled for release in 2020 or 2021 was delayed by the unceasing and ever-changing nature of the pandemic. One such dynamic existed amongst fans of the James Bond film franchise, who had been expecting the 25th Bond film, *No Time to Die*, to premiere worldwide in April of 2020.

"Bond fandom" is an umbrella term that could capture any self-identified fan of the James Bond franchise, but membership, as it were, is often associated with individuals who enjoy watching the film series, and doing so across multiple eras of the six men who have played the role of Bond in Eon productions: Sean Connery (1962-71), George Lazenby (1969), Roger Moore (1973-85), Timothy Dalton (1987-89), Pierce Brosnan (1995-2002), and Daniel Craig (2006-21). While the James Bond novels and short stories written by Ian Fleming between 1954 and 1966 were consumed by a modest-sized audience in the UK and U.S. upon release, the franchise became a popular culture phenomenon in the 1960s when they were adapted into spy-action films starring Connery (Chapman 15). Beginning with *Dr. No*, the Bond films were increasingly exhibited on cinema screens around the world and quickly inspired a global fan base for the British secret agent equipped with a '00' license to kill (Chapman 56). Between 1962 and 2015, the franchise spawned a successful string of 24 "must see" blockbusters whose releases became popular culture events in and of themselves. These releases, especially in modern times, often came with strong opening weekend box office numbers as both fans of the franchise and casual moviegoers alike flocked to see 007 in action ("Box Office History").

Bond film fandom is transnational, given the global popularity of the series, but also multi-generational, given that the 25 films by Eon Productions were released across a 59-year period. This accounts for a wide range in preferences across Bond fans for actors, films, and eras, and contributes to fan engagements surrounding the "best" and "worst" aspects of the film series. Bond fandom also encompasses those who enjoy the James Bond novels and short stories written by Fleming (1953-66), the James Bond continuation novels written by authors after Fleming, licensed comics and video games, and the *James Bond Jr.* (1991-92) cartoon series, among other official texts.

Additionally, Bond fandom not only includes the consumption of content and one's preferences and tastes regarding it, but also can capture the ways through which some engage with said culture beyond viewing or reading. This might mean, but is not limited to: publicly expressing "love" for the series; collecting merchandise/memorabilia; learning about the history of the texts and their production; repeated engagement with texts; emulation of style, actions, and dialogue; traveling to shooting destinations (i.e., Bond tourism); development of fan culture such as art, short stories, graphic novels, podcasts, and videos; and/or social media engagement. As Claire Hines notes, "new media technologies have enabled new forms of interaction, circulation and creative expressions and appropriation that directly impact on both Bond fan culture and aspects of the existing Bond mythos" (Hines 5).

Fandom played a critical role in shaping the discourse surrounding the production and eventual release of the *No Time to Die*, the 25th film in the series. There was popular (both media and fan-driven) discussion surrounding delays in production of Bond 25 well before COVID, often focused on the cycling in (e.g., Phoebe Waller-Bridge as scriptwriter) and out (e.g., Danny Boyle as director) of creative filmmaking personnel (Haynes). Additionally, there was speculation as to how casting and characterization would provide continuity (e.g., Daniel Craig returning for his last installment) and change (e.g., Lashana Lynch playing an agent with the code 007) throughout the latest entry into the canon (Collis; Funnell; Harmon). Finally, following Craig's revelation that Bond 25 would be his swan song in the lead role, there was extensive debate as to who should replace him, whether it was time for the character to evolve, what such evolution might look like, and whether there was space for a James Bond that was in any way different from what the public expected (Bruney; Charles; Johnson and Funnell 251; Mackelden; Sippell). While these conversations ranged from supportive to combative, they fueled consistent mainstream and social media engagement for fans as they awaited a long-anticipated release slated for April of 2020.

However, the element that had the greatest impact on fan discourse leading up to the eventual release of *No Time to Die* was the global pandemic. While the film was delayed twice pre-COVID due to production issues, it was the first major film to alter its release strategy due to the onset of the pandemic, with producers deciding in early March of 2020 to shift the release to November of that year (Whitten). This sudden cancellation of the premiere due to health and safety issues emerging from the global spread of COVID was met with a range of reactions, many positive but some negative. Even before producers made their decision to postpone, prominent fan sites like MI6-HQ suggested that public health should be top priority and that the public could wait a bit longer for 007's return (Murphy). This open letter was well received in the press (who promoted the "safety first" position widely), but a few in the public directed anger toward the contributors, sending hate mail and even death threats in response to this proactive stance (Page, "0043: Social Distancing"). Unsurprisingly, some fans were merely disappointed by yet another delay in the film's release, while others who had planned to attend the premiere in London and other cities had to request refunds for their tickets (Milan).

One byproduct of the 19-month delay in the film's release was a strengthening of Bond fandom for some, which was facilitated in part by social media. During this time of crisis, people not only binge watched new tv shows as they isolated/quarantined at home (Horeck 35; Sigre-Leirós et al. 2), but also often consumed their favorite media texts (such as Bond films) as a coping mechanism, a cultural "comfort food" so to speak (Bradshaw). This period saw the rise of new Bond influencers leading Bond watch parties on Twitter, holding Zoom events for fans to connect, producing and sharing videos, and starting up podcasts, the latter of which proliferated the most during this time. Nostalgia for the series, in the era of COVID, helped to deepen fan connection and resulted in an increased appetite for any/all things Bond 25, including new promotional materials, the release of the new Bond song, and any drop of information being slowly released from the franchise's producers (e.g., Page, "0088: Lock Down A-Z"). Much of the positive energy surrounding Bond during this time was bound to a sense of hopefulness that the release of the Bond film would constitute a return to normality—that COVID would end soon, and the public could go back to the way things were, with going to the movies being a part of that.

Amidst this groundswell of fan fervor, the lodestar for those who loved Bond and the interactions they had in virtual spaces remained *No Time to Die*, the release of which remained continuously impacted by different waves of COVID and levels of infection that fluctuated around the world. What was promised for April 2020 became November 2020 and

April 2021, and with each passing delay fans were forced to adapt to an uncertain how and when of a global release for the film. This also resulted in uncertainty for producers and industry insiders as to whether the lure of the latest Bond film was enough to draw fans back to the theater, at what point, and under what conditions. It is this uncertainty that public opinion research can offer greater insight into.

METHODOLOGY AND DATA

To examine how risk assessments during COVID-19, ideology, and fandom shaped projected willingness to see films (and, more specifically, *No Time to Die*) in the theater, an original survey was conducted.[1] 2,067 American individuals participated via Lucid from May 21-22, 2021.[2] This time frame captured the lowest point in positive COVID cases and deaths in nearly a year, as well as a moment at which just over half the population had received at least one dose of a vaccine ("Coronavirus: United States"; "Coronavirus (COVID-19) Vaccinations").[3]

After consenting to take part in the survey, respondents were asked about the frequency with which they saw movies in a theater before the COVID-19 pandemic. 25% were not theatergoers at all, 32% saw 1-3 movies in the theater per year, another 20% saw 4-6, and the remaining 23% saw 7 or more. The sample was then given a list of film franchises and the opportunity to characterize their fandom of these series on a 2-point scale, declaring whether they were or were not a fan.

---

1   Survey questions used in statistical models in this manuscript can be found in the Appendix.

2   Lucid samples approximate being nationally representative in terms of age, ethnicity, gender, and region.

3   The implications of the timing of this survey are discussed later in this manuscript.

This self-identification approach offers insight into how the public sees themselves, eliminating any gatekeeping around fandom of the franchises of interest. One of these franchises asked about was the James Bond film franchise; of the 2,067 participants, just over half (1,134, or 55%) stated they were a fan of Bond.[4]

Respondents proceeded to answer a series of questions related to the then-upcoming October 2021 release of *No Time to Die* and their general willingness to set foot in a movie theater in the near future. One of these questions asked about the situation in which they were likely to see *No Time to Die,* with response categories capturing if, where, when, and under what COVID-related protocols like social distancing. At one end of the scale, 30% of the sample had no plans to see the film, and another 36% said they were most likely to see it at home via cable television or a streaming service following its time in the theater. At the other end of the scale, 10% were likely to see it opening weekend, with slightly less than half of those individuals stating they would see it then even without social distancing measures in place. Participants were asked to consider their interest in seeing any movie in a theater in the next few months if social distancing measures were not in place. On a scale from 0 to 10, nearly half of respondents were between 0-3 when it comes to such interest. Just under 12% placed themselves at a 10 in this scale.

---

4   These are not used as variables in the forthcoming statistical models, but other survey questions asked to respondents determined that 49% saw themselves as "interested" or "highly interested" in the Bond franchise (with 26% "disinterested" or "highly disinterested"), while 15% had never seen a Bond film, 30% had seen 1-3, 23% had seen 4-6, 11% had seen 7-9, and 20% had seen 10 or more of the 24 films. These measures are all positively correlated at moderate levels (between .51 and .64) with the "self-identification" fandom measure used in the models.

Following the completion of this set of questions on movie-going, the survey experience closed with a battery of demographic, political, and social questions. This offers a bit more insight into just exactly who makes up the survey sample. In terms of demographics, 23% were between the ages of 18 and 29, while another 16% were 65 or older. 69% selected "White" as their sole racial or ethnic identity. 48% identified as male. 35% had a bachelor's degree or higher. 88% did not identify as gay, lesbian, or bisexual. 47% made less than $40,000 a year. 35% described the place where they lived as urban, while 22% chose rural. In terms of politics and society, 34% were liberal, 34% moderate, and 33% conservative, while 41% identified as Democrats, 31% as independents, and 28% as Republicans. 34% got news on a daily basis from newspapers, television, the internet, or podcasts, while 40% did the same via social media sites like Facebook and Twitter. Finally, and most central to the research questions explored here, 44% thought at that time that the coronavirus pandemic was a crisis, 47% thought it was a problem but not a crisis, and 9 percent felt it was not a problem at all.

FINDINGS

An initial set of analyses examines the effects of COVID (as well as other demographic, political, and social predictors) on individual interest in going to the theater without social distancing in place in the next few months. The dependent variable here ranges from 0-10; given that this measure has a limited set of categories with a clear order to it, this model uses ordered logit regression. Alternate specifications relying on ordinary least squares (OLS) regression show no differences in terms of sign or significance. Results can be found in Table 1.

Table 1: Effect of COVID on theatergoing "in the next few months"

	Interest in going without social distancing	
COVID a crisis?	-0.51*	(0.06)
Theatergoing History	0.32*	(0.03)
Age	-0.02*	(0.00)
Race (White=1)	-0.03	(0.09)
Sexuality (Straight=1)	0.27*	(0.12)
Sex (Male=1)	0.25*	(0.08)
Education	0.01	(0.02)
Area	-0.09	(0.06)
Income	0.02	(0.03)
Party Identification	0.06	(0.06)
Ideology	0.06*	(0.03)
Social Media News	0.06*	(0.02)
Mainstream Media News	-0.07*	(0.02)

Ordered logit model. N=2,063. * = $p < .05$. Pseudo R-squared = .04.

As is evident from the first row of this table, there is a strong relationship between attitudes on whether COVID is a crisis and interest in going to the theater in the next few months without social distancing. This relationship is also in the expected direction, with those who perceive COVID as a crisis less interested in social distancing-free theatergoing in the near future. As ordered logit coefficients are not directly interpretable beyond sign and significance, one can analyze their meaning by considering them in terms of predicted probabilities. The probability of an individual who believes COVID is a crisis being a 10 out of 10 on the idea of interest in returning to the theater in the next few months without social distancing is only 7%; this rises to 11% if they see COVID as a problem but not a crisis, and 17% if they feel COVID is not a problem at all.[5] The probability of an individual who believes COVID is a crisis being a 0 out of 10 on the idea of interest in returning to the theater in the next few months without social distancing is 27%; this falls to 18% if they see COVID as a problem but not a crisis, and 12% if they feel COVID is not a problem at all. These results fit with work from early in the pandemic that showed how individual assessments of the state of the pandemic predicted how seriously one took restrictions on activity. Unsurprisingly though, individuals who had a history of seeing films in the theater before the pandemic are more likely to report an interest in returning soon without social distancing. Respondents who saw 13 or more movies per year in the theater pre-pandemic had a 27% probability of being at a 10 out

---

5   Predicted probabilities throughout this section are derived using the Margins function in STATA; all other variables are set at their means. Previous work (e.g., Funnell and Johnson 111; Johnson and Funnell 251) does show that knowledge of the Bond franchise and number of Bond films seen are inconsistent predictors of attitudes toward the franchise itself.

of 10 on the idea of returning to the theater in the next few months without social distancing, while those who only saw 1-3 per year were at 8% probability.

There is also clear evidence (via significance and sign) that demographics and information gathering predict who is more or less likely to be interested in returning to the movie theater in the next few months without social distancing in place. Males are more likely to be interested in doing so than females (which is expected given literature cited earlier), and gay, lesbian, or bisexual participants are less likely than those who identify as straight. Older individuals were less likely to be interested in doing so than younger ones. Conservatives were more likely to be interested than liberals, which aligns with the broader politics of COVID restrictions. Fascinatingly, the more regularly an individual relies on social media for news, the more likely they are to express interest in returning to the theater in the near future without distancing, but the same cannot be said for those who rely on newspapers, television, the internet, or podcasts. The more regularly an individual consumed news these ways, the less likely they were to report being interested in returning to moviegoing without distancing in the next few months. Such findings may offer insight into what is being learned where.

Given this base level of knowledge about habits, how might fandom of a specific film franchise with an upcoming release scheduled shape one's specific plans to consume new franchise content? In Table 2, several more independent variables are added to the set from the previous model: whether or not a respondent reported being a fan of James Bond, and an interaction term between this variable and whether an individual felt COVID was a crisis, a problem but not a crisis, or not a problem at all. This interaction will determine

Table 2: Effect of fandom and COVID assessment on
seeing *No Time to Die*

	Opening weekend with no social distancing	
Bond Fan?	2.53*	(0.34)
COVID a crisis?	0.11	(0.11)
Fan*Crisis	-0.27*	(0.14)
Theatergoing History	0.34*	(0.03)
Age	-0.02*	(0.00)
Race (White=1)	-0.14	(0.10)
Sexuality (Straight=1)	-0.01	(0.13)
Sex (Male=1)	0.38*	(0.09)
Education	0.08*	(0.03)
Area	0.00	(0.04)
Income	-0.00	(0.03)
Party Identification	-0.07	(0.06)
Ideology	0.01	(0.03)
Social Media News	0.01	(0.02)
Mainstream Media News	0.04	(0.02)

Ordered logit model. N=2,063. * = $p < .05$. Pseudo R-squared = 0.13.

whether Bond fans who see COVID as a crisis differ in their outlook on when and how to see *No Time to Die* from those who see it as a problem or not a problem at all. The dependent variable here captures plans (or lack thereof) to see *No Time to Die* on a 6-point scale, ranging from "I do not plan to see this film" to "in the theater opening weekend, even if no social distancing measures are taken." Since this variable has distinct categories that progress in a direction, once again ordered logit modeling is utilized to tease out statistical relationships.

Unsurprisingly, Bond fandom is a powerful and positive predictor of who was likely to see *No Time to Die* opening weekend no matter what interventions might not be undertaken by a theater in the midst of a pandemic. Predicted probabilities reveal that self-identified Bond fans were over 11 times more likely than those who did not identify as fans to say they would see *No Time to Die* opening weekend even if no social distancing measures were taken. Interestingly though, this relationship is reversed when the fandom variable is interacted with the variable considering whether a respondent felt COVID was a crisis. The effect here is negative and significant, illustrating how perceptions of the state of the pandemic conditioned the desire of fans to see the film as soon as possible no matter the precautions. Bond fans who thought COVID was a crisis were less likely to believe they would be in the theater opening weekend even without social distancing than fans who thought COVID was a problem but not a crisis or fans who thought COVID was no problem at all. In terms of predicted probabilities, Bond fans who thought COVID was a crisis were 1.7 times less likely to see the film in the theater opening weekend even if no social distancing measures were in place than Bond fans who thought COVID was no problem at all.

There are some similarities in terms of significance between Tables 1 and 2 when it comes to demographics as well. Older individuals were less likely than younger ones to believe they would see *No Time to Die* opening weekend even without social distancing. The same goes for females. Other predictors of behavior on this question included pre-COVID moviegoing habits and education, with regular theatergoers and the highly educated more likely to see the film early and no matter the conditions than those who saw films in person less frequently and the less educated. Unlike in Table 1, sexuality, political ideology, and media consumption habits had no relationship with plans to see the latest James Bond film.

CONCLUSIONS AND FUTURE DIRECTIONS

The findings here illustrate, in general fashion, the ways in which the COVID pandemic and assessments of its severity played a role in shaping the public's plans to return to public spaces like the movie theater. Individuals who perceived the pandemic to be a crisis were less likely to see themselves going to the movies in the near future without social distancing precautions taken than those who only saw it as a problem or did not see it as a problem at all. These findings offer further evidence, this time in relation to the entertainment sector, that an individual's perception of the current state of COVID was key in predicting their willingness to take on risk. When one looks more specifically at the James Bond film franchise, its fandom, and an upcoming and highly anticipated event (i.e., the release of *No Time to Die* in theaters) for those taking this survey in May of 2021, one discovers COVID's ability to condition the behavior of individuals who we would assume to be clamoring to see the film at the earliest availability under circumstances that resembled pre-pandemic moviegoing. Fandom in general predicted a higher likelihood of seeing the film opening weekend even without social distancing in place; however, fans who still believed COVID was a crisis were less likely to see themselves as rushing into the local cinema without social distancing measures in the first few days the movie had opened.

The fact that fandom can be overcome by aversion to risk has implications for the entertainment industry across future crises or disasters. Fans cannot necessarily be counted on to show up at points where they perceive risk to be present. What is less clear (and unable to be answered by this survey) is whether COVID-19 is unique in its power to have such effects, or if other types of disasters would reshape fandom in such fashion. Perhaps future experimental research could test situations that might cause passionate supporters of specific film franchises, sporting teams, or musicians to think twice about attending a live event versus finding an alternate path to consume such content. It is also difficult to determine how the timing of the survey shaped outcomes and whether the findings would shift in any noticeable fashion if it had been conducted six months earlier (before the vaccine became ubiquitous) or six months later (when the Delta variant of COVID had come to dominate and the Omicron variant was about to take root). In some ways, the fact that there were relationships between assessments of COVID, fandom, and projected moviegoing behavior at a low point of severity during the pandemic suggests that such effects might be even more powerful at points where public panic was more pronounced. This cannot be known for certain, however, and barring new waves of the pandemic (or different future pandemics) it cannot be tested. As such, it is left for speculation. Finally, it is possible that choices made regarding how to measure fandom might shape what can be taken away from the findings presented here. The statistical models in this research use the most inclusive measure of fandom possible: self-identification. Perhaps far more restrictive measures (e.g., having reached a specific high threshold in terms of number of films seen, individual propensity to take part in franchise-related activities outside of seeing the films, or the ability to exhibit knowledge of Bond facts) would spur similar or different findings. One could envision that a more restrictive measure of who was a fan could have greater predictive power as to who would see *No Time to Die* in traditional fashion, but weaker predictive power when interacted with assessments of COVID. The responses to such hypothetical questions remain unknown (but provide potential fodder for future survey research on fandom).[6]

Where there is no need for speculation, however, is when it comes to the fate *No Time to Die* met at the box office in the fall and winter of 2021. As the COVID-19 pandemic progressed, there was plenty of talk in the media about how the film industry was being impacted, with many cinemas and theater chains closing, film releases being pushed back, and even the fear that cinema, as we know it, might die. These concerns were matched with the promotion of the idea that Bond could save cinema just like the character in the film saves the world from imminent destruction (Nelson). As noted by Erik David, managing editor of Fandango.com, James Bond is "one of the biggest global properties that exists right now in the theatrical space" and had the greatest chance of being a blockbuster hit of all films delayed by COVID (Gilblom).

But for Bond to save cinema, it would require the average person to brave the risks of COVID to view the film in the

---

6   Previous work (e.g. Funnell and Johnson 111; Johnson and Funnell 251) does show that knowledge of the Bond franchise and number of Bond films seen are inconsistent predictors of attitudes toward the franchise itself.

theater, as *No Time to Die* had an exclusive theatrical release; this strategy set the film apart from other anticipated blockbusters like *Wonder Woman 1984* and *Black Widow*, which had streaming or hybrid (simultaneous theater/streaming) options (Gilblom). This theater-only option was not only true to the Bond brand but also a reflection of the financial toll that delays had taken on the production company MGM, which accrued a significant amount of debt over time (Fuge). As a result, the rhetoric surrounding Bond saving cinema was less about the industry and more about the profitability of a particular company and relied strongly on the willingness of fans and filmgoers to be like Bond and take calculated risks to see *No Time to Die* in public.

The film earned over $770 million USD at the worldwide box-office and was the third highest grossing Bond film of the Daniel Craig era, with 2012's *Skyfall* earning over $1 billion USD and 2015's *Spectre* making $880 million USD ("Box Office History"). *No Time to Die* was also one of the top grossing films of 2021 until the release of *Spiderman: No Way Home* surpassed it, earning over $1.8 billion USD globally ("2021 Worldwide Box Office"). However, opening weekend box office numbers in the United States were "slightly behind projections," with the film making $56 million USD, about 5-15 million less than industry insiders anticipated (Rubin). Moreover, the film needed to earn $900 million USD in order to break even, a feat that according to *Variety*, "would have been realistic had a global health crisis not upended the theater industry" resulting in reluctance on the part of adult audiences, who constitute the target market for *No Time to Die*, to return to the cinema (Rubin and Lang). As a result, the film was strategically released for digital rental on November 9—only one month after the US theatrical release—and was available on Blu-ray and DVD on December 20 just in time for Christmas 2021. This was a way for producers to quickly maximize profits during the pandemic by opening at-home options to those who were reluctant to see the film in theaters. In the end, it appears that while the prospect of seeing James Bond's latest adventure as immediately as possible scared the living daylights out of some, enough moviegoers made it to the theater over time to allow the film to begin to approach profitability.

WORKS CITED

"2021 Worldwide Box Office." *Box Office Mojo*, 2021, https://www.boxofficemojo.com/year/world/2021/

Adgate, Brad. "The Impact COVID-19 Had on the Entertainment Industry in 2020." *Forbes*, 21 Apr 2021, https://www.forbes.com/sites/bradadgate/2021/04/13/the-impact-covid-19-had-on-the-entertainment-industry-in-2020/?sh=6d365223250f

Andrews, Penny. "Receipts, Radicalisation, Reactionaries, and Repentance: The Digital Dissensus, Fandom, and the COVID-19 Pandemic." *Feminist Media Studies*, vol. 20, 2020, pp. 902-907.

Bauer, Raymond. "Consumer Behavior as Risk Taking." *Dynamic Marketing for a Changing World*, edited by Robert Hancock, American Marketing Association, 1960, pp. 389-398.

Black Widow. Directed by Cate Shortland, Marvel Studios, 2021.

"Box Office History for James Bond Movies." The Numbers, 2022, https://www.the-numbers.com/movies/franchise/James-Bond#tab=summary

Bradshaw, Peter. "Comfort Films to Watch While Self-Isolating – Ranked!" *The Guardian,* 12 Mar. 2020, https://www.theguardian.com/film/2020/mar/12/comfort-films-to-watch-while-self-isolating-coronavirus-ranked

Briscese, Guglielmo, Nicola Lacetera, Mario Macis, and Mirco Tonin. 2020. *Expectations, reference points, and compliance with COVID-19 social distancing measures.* National Bureau of Economic Research: 26916.

Bruney, Gabrielle. "Billie Eilish Thinks Michael B. Jordan Should Be the Next Bond." *Esquire,* 23 Feb. 2020, https://www.esquire.com/entertainment/tv/a31065108/billie-eilish-james-bond-michael-b-jordan/

Cameron, Lisa and Manisha Shah. "Risk-Taking Behavior in the Wake of Natural Disasters." *Journal of Human Resources,* vol. 50, 2015, pp. 484-515.

Chapman, James. *Licence to Thrill: A Cultural History of the James Bond Films.* IB Tauris, 2007.

Charles, Douglas. "Movie Fans React to Daniel Craig Saying the Next James Bond Should Not Be a Woman." *Brobible,* 21 Sept. 2021, https://brobible.com/culture/article/daniel-craig-james-bond-not-woman/

Collis, Clark. "Daniel Craig Confirms He's 'Done' with James Bond Franchise." *Entertainment Weekly,* 23 Nov. 2019, https://ew.com/movies/2019/11/23/daniel-craig-james-bond/

"Coronavirus: United States." *Worldometers,* 2022, https://www.worldometers.info/coronavirus/country/us/

"Coronavirus (COVID-19) Vaccinations." *Our World In Data,* 2022, https://ourworldindata.org/covid-vaccinat

ions?country=USA

Dr. No. Directed by Terence Young, Eon Productions, 1962.

Fuge, Jonathan. "No Time to Die Delay is Costing MGM Nearly $1 Million a Month in Interest." *Movieweb.com,* 29 Oct. 2020, https://movieweb.com/james-bond-no-time-to-die-delay-interest-costs/

Funnell, Lisa. "Nomi/No Me? Race, gender, and power in *No Time To Die*." *Flow Journal*, 2019, https://www.flowjournal.org/2019/09/nomi-no-me/

Funnell, Lisa, and Tyler Johnson. "Properties of a Lady: Public Perceptions of Women in the

James Bond Franchise." *Participations*, vol. 17, 2020, pp. 95-114.

Gilblom, Kelly. "James Bond Becomes Theatres' New Hope for a Box Office Jolt." *Bloomberg,* 1

October 2021, https://www.bloomberg.com/news/articles/2021-10-01/james-bond-becomes-theaters-newest-hope-for-a-box-office-jolt

Griffith, Derek M., et al. "Men and COVID-19: A Biopsychosocial Approach to Understanding Sex Differences in Mortality and Recommendations for Practice and Policy Interventions." *Preventing Chronic Disease*, vol. 17, 2020, pp. E63.

Harmon, Steph. "Bond's Number Is Up: Black Female Actor 'Is the New 007.'" *The Guardian*, 15 July 2019, https://www.theguardian.com/film/2019/jul/15/lashana-lynch-new-007-james-bond-daniel-craig

Harper, Craig A., et al. "Functional Fear Predicts Public Health Compliance in the COVID-19 Pandemic." *International Journal of Mental Health and Addiction*, vol. 19, 2021, pp. 1875-1888.

Haynes, Suyin. "A Guide to the Many Setbacks That Have Plagued the Production of the Bond Movie 'No Time to Die.'" *Time*, 22 Jul. 2019, https://time.com/5627267/bond-25-production-troubles/

Hines, Claire. "Introduction." *Fan Phenomena: James Bond*, edited by Claire Hines, Intellect, 2015, pp. 5-9.

Horeck, Tanya. "'Netflix and Heal': The Shifting Meanings of Binge-Watching During the Covid-19 Crisis." *Film Quarterly*, vol. 75, issue 1, 2021, pp. 35-40.

Johnson, Tyler, and Lisa Funnell. "Nobody Does It Better: Identity, Ideology, and the Future of James Bond." *Social Science Quarterly*, vol. 103, issue 2, 2022, pp. 245-258.

Keinan, Ruty, et al. "Compliance with COVID-19 Prevention Guidelines: Active vs. Passive Risk Takers." *Judgment & Decision Making*, vol. 16, 2021, pp. 20-35.

Linden, Henrik and Sara Linden. *Fans and Fan Cultures: Tourism, Consumerism, and Social Media*. London: Palgrave Macmillan, 2017.

Mackelden, Amy. "Harry Styles Is Not the Next James Bond, So Just Cancel the Franchise Already." *Harper's Bazaar*, 3 Oct, 2020, https://www.harpersbazaar.com/celebrity/latest/a34257703/harry-styles-james-bond-007-replacement/

Mastromartino, Brandon, et al. "Thinking Outside the 'Box':

A Discussion of Sports Fans, Teams, and the Environment in the Context of COVID-19." *Sport in Society*, vol. 23, 2020, pp. 1707-1723.

Milan, Aidan. "What To Do If You've Bought Tickets to See James Bond as *No Time to Die* Release Date Pushed Back." *Metro*, 4 Mar. 2020, https://metro.co.uk/2020/03/04/bought-tickets-see-james-bond-no-time-die-release-date-pushed-back-12349805/

Moorhouse, H.F. *Driving Ambitions: An Analysis of the American Hot Rod Enthusiasm,* Manchester University Press, 1991.

Murphy, J. Kim. "James Bond Fan Site Urges For 'No Time to Die' Release Delay Due To Coronavirus." *Variety*, 2 Mar. 2020, https://variety.com/2020/film/news/james-bond-fan-site-no-time-to-die-coronavirus-1203521114/

Nelson, Eshe. "James Bond Saved the World, but Can He Rescue U.K. Movie Theaters?" *The New York Times*, 6 Oct. 2021, https://www.nytimes.com/2021/10/06/movies/no-time-to-die-uk.html

No Time to Die. Directed by Cary Fukuaga, MGM/Eon Productions, 2021.

Outreville, J. François. "Risk Aversion, Risk Behavior, and Demand for Insurance: A Survey." *Journal of Insurance Issues*, vol. 37, 2014, pp.158-186.

Page, James. "0043: Social Distancing." *James Bond & Friends,* 6 Mar. 2020, https://podcast.mi6-hq.com/e/0043-social-distancing/

——. "0088: Lock Down A-Z." *James Bond & Friends.* 29

Apr. 2021, https://podcast.mi6-hq.com/e/0088-lock-down-a-z/

Pantano, Eleonora, et al. "Tweets to Escape: Intercultural Differences in Consumer Expectations and Risk Behavior During the COVID-19 Lockdown in Three European Countries." *Journal of Business Research*, vol. 130, 2021, pp.59-69.

Rubin, Rebecca. "'Black Widow' Release Pulled Amongst Coronavirus Pandemic." *Variety*, 17 May 2020, https://variety.com/2020/film/box-office/black-widow-release-coronavirus-1203532996/

———. "Box Office: 'No Time to Die' Debuts Slightly Behind Expectations with $56 Million." *Variety*, 10 Oct. 2021, https://variety.com/2021/film/box-office/box-office-no-time-to-die-opening-weekend-daniel-craig-1235085585/

Rubin, Rebecca and Brent Lang. "Covid-Era Conundrum: 'No Time to Die' May Be the Year's

Highest-Grossing Hollywood Movie, But It Could Still Lose Millions." *Variety*, 22 November 2021, https://variety.com/2021/film/news/no-time-to-die-highest-grossing-movie-losing-money-blockbusters-1235111919/

Ryu, Sunghan, and Daegon Cho. "The Show Must Go on? The Entertainment Industry during (and after) COVID-19." *Media, Culture & Society*, vol. 44, 2022, pp. 591-600.

Sheth, Jagdish. "Impact of Covid-19 on Consumer Behavior: Will the Old Habits Return or Die?" *Journal of Business Research*, vol. 117, 2020, pp. 280-283.

Sigre-Leirós, Vera et al. "Binge-Watching in Time of Covid-19: A Longitudinal Examination of Changes in Affect and TV Series Consumption Patterns During Lockdown." *Psychology of Popular Media*, forthcoming.

Sippell, Margeaux. *"No Time to Die* Hasn't Even Hit Theaters and Twitter is Already Having a Field Day with the Next Bond." *Moviemaker,* 29 Sept. 2021, https://www.moviemaker.com/no-time-to-die-twitter-field-day-next-james-bond/

Skyfall. Directed by Sam Mendes, MGM/Eon Productions, 2012.

Solomou, Ioulia, and Fofi Constantinidou. "Prevalence and Predictors of Anxiety and Depression Symptoms During the COVID-19 Pandemic and Compliance with Precautionary Measures: Age and Sex Matter." *International Journal of Environmental Research and Public Health*, vol. 17, 2020, pp. 1-19.

Spectre. Directed by Sam Mendes, MGM/Eon Productions, 2015.

Spider-Man: No Way Home. Directed by Jon Watts, Marvel Studios, 2021.

Taylor, James. "The Role of Risk in Consumer Behavior: A Comprehensive and Operational Theory of Risk Taking in Consumer Behavior." *Journal of Marketing,* vol. 38, 1974, pp. 54-60.

Tulloch, John and Henry Jenkins. *Science Fiction Audiences: Watching Doctor Who and Star* Trek. Routledge, 1995.

Whitten, Sarah. "James Bond Movie 'No Time to Die' Release

Delayed Until November Due to Coronavirus." *CNBC*, 4 Mar. 2020, https://www.cnbc.com/2020/03/04/james-
-bond-movie-no-time-to-die-release-delayed-due-to-co
ronavirus.html

Wonder Woman 1984. Directed by Patty Jenkins, Warner Bros. Pictures, 2020.

Zajenkowski, Marcin, et al. "Who Complies with the Restrictions to Reduce the Spread of COVID-19? Personality and Perceptions of the COVID-19 Situation." *Personality and Individual Differences*, vol. 166, 2020, 110199.

Appendix: Survey Questions

Note: questions below are as they appeared in the survey but do not necessarily represent how variables were constructed in the models. For more information on the survey and variables, please consult the authors.

Theatergoing History: Prior to the COVID-19 pandemic, approximately how many movies would you see in a theater/cinema each year? A) 0, B) 1-3, C) 4-6, D) 7-9, E) 10-12, F) 13 or more

Bond Fan: How would you characterize your fandom of...? James Bond? A) I am not a fan, B) I am a fan

Seeing *NTTD*: The latest James Bond film, *No Time to Die*, is scheduled to be released in theaters on October 8, 2021. In which situation, if any, are you likely to see this film? A) I do not plan to see this film, B) At home via cable television or a streaming service (e.g., Netflix, Amazon Prime) following its time in the theater, C) In the theater at some point after opening weekend, but only if social distancing measures are taken, D) In the theater at some point after opening weekend, even if no social distancing measures are taken, E) In the theater opening weekend, but only if social distancing measures are taken, F) In the theater opening weekend, even if no social distancing measures are taken

Seeing any movie: How interested are you in seeing any movie in a theater in the next few months under the following conditions: Without social distancing measures in place? A) 0, B) 1, C) 2, D) 3, E) 4, F) 5, G) 6, H) 7, I) 8, J) 9, K) 10.

Age: How old are you? (Number entered in box)

Race: What is your race? Select all that apply. A) American Indian/Native American, B) Asian American/Pacific Islander, C) Black/African American, D) Latino/Hispanic, E) White, F) Other

Education: What is the highest level of education you have completed? A) Some high school, no diploma, B) High school, C) Some college, no diploma, D) Associates or other 2-year degree, E) Bachelor's or other 4-year degree, F) Some post-graduate coursework, no post-graduate diploma, G) Post-graduate degree (examples: MA, MBA, MD, MPA, JD, PhD)

Sex: What is your sex? A) Male, B) Female, C) Nonbinary/Third

Sexuality: Do you identify as gay, lesbian, or bisexual? A) No, B) Yes, C) Unsure

Income: Which of the following categories best captures your total combined household income in 2020 before taxes? A) Under $20,000, B) $20,000-$39,999, C) $40,000-$59,999, D) $60,000-$79,999, E) $80,000-$99,999, F) $100,000-$199,999, G) $200,000 or above

Area: Which of the following best describes the area you live in? A) Urban, B) Suburban, C) Rural

Media: On average, how often do you read the news section of a newspaper, watch news coverage on television, read news content on the internet, or listen to news-related podcasts? A) Never, B) Less than once a month, C) Once a month, D) 2-3 times a month, E) Once a week, F) 2-3 times a week, G) Every day

Social Media: How often do you use social media (e.g., Facebook, Twitter) to get your news? A) Never, B) Less than once a month, C) Once a month, D) 2-3 times a month, E) Once a week, F) 2-3 times a week, G) Every day

Ideology: Where would you place yourself on a scale from very liberal to very conservative? A) Very liberal, B) Liberal, C) Slightly liberal, D) Moderate, E) Slightly conservative, F) Conservative, G) Very conservative

Party Identification: Generally speaking, do you usually think of yourself as a Democrat, a Republican, or an Independent? A) Democrat, B) Independent, C) Republican

COVID: At the moment, do you think that the coronavirus pandemic in the United States is a crisis, a problem but not a crisis, or not a problem at all? A) A crisis, B) A problem but not a crisis, C) Not a problem at all

The Disease Becomes the Host: Cattle Decapitation's Pandemic Discourse from Song to Music Video

. . . .

By Anna Marini and Michael Fuchs

ABSTRACT

On April 2, 2020, extreme metal band Cattle Decapitation released a video for their song "Bring Back the Plague" (2019), whose lyrics invoke a pandemic that wipes out humanity as a means to counter the anthropogenic devastation of Earth. This article explores these lyrics vis-à-vis the music video, which tackles the spatiotemporal disruption caused by stay-at-home orders at the onset of the COVID-19 pandemic, condemning anomic behavior and appealing to solidarity and social responsibility.

Keywords: COVID-19, coronavirus, pandemics, metal music, music video, Anthropocene

Email address for correspondence: annamarta.marini@gmail.com

La enfermedad se convierte en el anfitrión: el discurso pandémico de la decapitación del ganado de la canción al video musical

RESUMEN

El 2 de abril de 2020, la banda de metal extremo Cattle Decapitation lanzó un video de su canción "Bring Back the Plague" (2019), cuya letra invoca una pandemia que acaba con la humanidad como un medio para contrarrestar la devastación antropogénica de la Tierra. Este artículo explora estas letras frente al video musical, que aborda la disrupción espaciotemporal provocada por las órdenes de quedarse en casa al inicio de la pandemia de COVID-19, condenando comportamientos anómalos y apelando a la solidaridad y la responsabilidad social.

Palabras clave: COVID-19, coronavirus, pandemias, Música metal, video musical, antropoceno

疾病成为宿主：Cattle Decapitation乐队从歌曲到音乐视频中的大流行话语

2020年4月2日，极端金属乐队Cattle Decapitation为他们的歌曲"Bring Back the Plague"（2019）发布了音乐视频，其歌词提到了一场消灭人类的大流行，以作为人为破坏地球的对抗手段。本文探究了这些歌词与音乐视频，该视频应对了2019冠状病毒病（COVID-19）大流行开始时居家令造成的时空中断，谴责了无规范的行为并呼吁团结和社会责任。

关键词：2019冠状病毒病，冠状病毒，大流行，金属音乐，音乐视频，人类世

---

n 2015, extracts from email exchanges between environmental philosopher Timothy Morton and singer/songwriter Björk were included in *Björk: Archives,* the catalog that accompanied a Björk retrospective at the Museum of Modern Art in New York. In one email, Morton explains that the song "Virus," included in Björk's album *Biophilia* (2011), is, in fact, a love song: "Being alive means being susceptible to viruses," Morton mused (Guðmundsdóttir and Morton),[1] embracing the "dark-sweet" character of human-virus entanglements (*Dark Ecology* 5). Two years later, Morton reflected on viral politics and stressed, "Claiming that the AIDS virus has as much right to exist as an AIDS patient is a conclusion you can draw within the logic of deep ecology, but it has nothing to do with actual ecological politics" ("Subscendence" para 4). Less than a month after President Trump had declared COVID-19 a national emergency, Morton continued reflecting on viruses and explained, "The Latin word *hostis* means host, guest, friend, enemy. Hospitality means you might open your door to a killer." They concluded that "[l]ife is a loose collective of uneasy alliances. Life is ambiguous. ... We just found out the hard way how humankind means solidarity with nonhuman people" ("Thank Virus" paras 4-7). But solidarity with viruses is fraught with incongruities. After all, viruses are "strange strangers" because they occupy the liminal space between life and death and they are simply so different from humans that they remain unfathomable entities (Morton, "Queer Ecology" 277). Nevertheless, Morton is strangely attracted to them: "I hate [the virus]. And I love it" ("Thank Virus" para 7). This expressly ambiguous attitude toward the coronavirus builds upon the difference between actual ecological politics and the logic of deep ecology Morton struggled with when discussing HIV, as humans are unable to imagine a world "so egalitarian that important human needs, such as health or survival, would not take priority" (Bennett 104).

---

1 Scott Snibbe, an interactive artist who designed the "app album" that accompanied the release of *Biophilia* noted in a 2011 interview with *The Guardian* that "Virus" is "a kind of love story between a virus and a cell. And of course the virus loves the cell so much that it destroys it" (Cragg para 4). Morton thus merely repeated discourse surrounding the album.

A similar discord defines the misanthropic, arguably deep-ecological lyrics performed by American extreme metal band Cattle Decapitation and the much less aggressive position taken in the music video for "Bring Back the Plague," in which they ultimately believe and foster confidence in human solidarity. Cattle Decapitation's oeuvre addresses environmental issues, in particular the negative consequences of human extractive and exploitative practices on the natural world. The environmental awareness performed in the songs was originally backed by a decidedly vegan lifestyle, but only two of the five current band members are vegetarian, in part due to the realities of touring on miniscule budgets. As frontman Travis Ryan has repeatedly stressed in interviews, there are definitive disagreements between their environmental agenda and routinely "burning fossil fuels" while touring the world.

"Bring Back the Plague" is part of the band's seventh studio album *Death Atlas*, which was released in fall 2019. The song draws on the idea of the "next pandemic," a cyclical space-time occurrence that humanity is destined to experience repeatedly until a final pandemic will wipe out humanity, whose existence on Earth "is simply not sustainable" ("Be Still Our Bleeding Hearts"). Upon the implementation of stay-at-home orders in the United States in spring 2020, an official music video was published on April 2, 2020, shot using amateur technology while the band was self-isolating. Since the lyrics of "Bring Back the Plague" could well have been interpreted as a possible call to ignore measures meant to contain the viral spread, the band evidently felt the need to comment on the pandemic unfolding in the real world. The music video accordingly critiques different responses to the pandemic through parody, while at the same time expressing the disorientation provoked by self-isolation and the influx of distressing news about the situation outside. In addition, it showcases the consequences of lockdown measures on professional musicians, resulting in an exemplary reflection on how the COVID-19 pandemic (in particular its early phase in spring 2020) altered people's perception of spatiotemporal and social existence.

The yearning for the extinction of *Homo sapiens* expressed in the lyrics thus clashed with the band's real-life political stance, enacted in a music video that engages with the inception of the COVID-19 pandemic in the United States. To be sure, in extreme metal, the transgression of norms is little more than a gesture (to riff on Foucault) and accordingly does not have any real-life consequences other than inducing a sense of shock and disgust (see Kahn-Harris 48–49). In other words, "thematic imagery is presented precisely as *theme*, that is, as meaning" rather than a call to action (van Ooijen 86). Nevertheless, the music video reflects the gap between the band's radically environmentalist rhetoric and their reaction to a concrete pandemic event. While their song "Vulturous" suggests a "need to see our species burning" to end human exploitation of the planet, the music video seems to embrace solidarity with other humans instead of "ditch[ing] the ignorant philanthropy" ("Be Still Our Bleeding Hearts").

DEATH ATLAS AND THE CHRONOTOPE OF RADICAL ENVIRONMENTALIST DISCOURSE

The Anthropocene conjuncture, its causes and effects, creates a multiplicity of new chronotopes and multipolar configurations that invite "Western-identified subjects to resituate themselves in the space-time-matter of the planet" (Pratt, "Coda" G170–G171). The Anthropocene discourse—and its multidimensional chronotopic unfoldings—is marked by

Popular Culture Review 33.1

a sense of irreversible threat that conveys a spatial and temporal absolute (Rothe 147–148), whose narratives tend to engage with apocalyptic scenarios of environmental destruction. The relevance of tracing space-time ecological patterns lies in the fact that human existence has been structured in ways that inevitably lead to the consumption, exploitation and destruction of the natural environment which, at the same time, endangers the survival of humankind (Müller 600).[2] As Madeleine Fagan indicates, climate change has been pervasively framed in terms of pressing disaster in both media commentary and popular culture (228–230); its urgency has both spatial and temporal implications that contribute to a sense of doom. Apocalyptic environmental discourse structures chronotopes that depend on temporal urgency, a near-future temporality that is palpable and "visible" (Bakhtin 84), but simultaneously connected to deep time through humanity's exploitation of fossil fuels and its indelible inscription into geological layers. Likewise, the space defined by this kind of narrative is marked by a global scope, and yet the imminence of environmental disaster situates it in a space of perceived vicinity. Such chronotopic interpretation is thus shaped by the telic perception of time and space connected to notions of irreversible temporal ending and the existential dread intrinsic to finitude.

---

2   Here, "human(kind)" refers to a "genre of the human" (Weheliye 2) that conforms to the "fundamental tenets of industrialism, including a ravenous appetite for consumption, the expectation of an ever-growing material standard of living, and a belief that all other forms of life exist to serve us" (Kidner 472). While various scholars have critiqued the human universalism inscribed into the very term "Anthropocene" (e.g. Yusoff, *Billion Black Anthropocenes*), we will replicate this problematic use because Cattle Decapitation's lyrics do not distinguish between different groups of humans—humanity is an "ecological tumor" and only the "[e]xtinction of man" can bring "peace on Earth," as they put it in their song "Everyone Deserves to Die" (2002).

Conceiving of the Anthropocene as a chronotope intersects with the proleptic characteristics of the chronotopes of memory, in which future experiences are anticipated based on past and present events, both temporally and spatially. Such structure permeates the proleptic patterns repeated throughout *Death Atlas*, revolving around the constant anticipation of human extinction. However, unlike the Anthropocene chronotope suggested by Mary Louise Pratt, which is characterized by humans "reimagining and remaking themselves in the space-time-matter of the planet and its beings" (*Planetary Longings* 121), the album seems to be trapped in a future imaginary that can barely see beyond the end of humankind.[3] After all, the lyrics employ an apocalyptic rhetoric that acknowledges the global, planetary scale of the environmental crisis underpinned by the relentless forward motion of time, irrevocably resulting in the annihilation of any space-time-matter configuration.

Opening with an instrumental track titled "Anthropogenic: End Transmission," *Death Atlas* is organized in four blocks, each of them introduced by an instrumental track. While "Anthropogenic: End Transmission" collects, as the title suggests, transmissions in different languages that point at the

---

3 Notably, the album's final song, "Death Atlas," oscillates between a timespace in which humankind "deserve[s] everything that's coming" and a timespace in which "[m]ankind [is] ... dead and gone" and in which "Earth [is] reset to day one." This is the only song that expressly mentions a "post-Anthropocene," which is, however, not a timespace thousands, if not millions of years, in the future, when human impact is no longer felt, but rather a timespace closely tied to the vanishing of humankind, demonstrating that the album is caught in anthropocentric and humanist discourses. To add a more positive spin to these textual inconsistencies, one might say that they are testament to the "bad environmentalism" defined by "contradiction, imperfection, and ambiguity" that Nicole Seymour has observed in popular environmental discourses (232).

end of the world, "The Great Dying," "The Great Dying II," and "The Unerasable Past" reference different environmental discourses. These three tracks stand out for the register employed, as they mention a few concrete issues related to the environmental crisis: the importance of bio-diverse regions, the sixth mass extinction, rising sea levels, and the "abnormal rises in upper-atmosphere methane levels" ("The Great Dying"; "The Unerasable Past"). Significantly, these three tracks are not songs but rather short intermezzos in which the entirety or at least parts of the text are delivered by distorted speaking voices. "The Great Dying" part one is spoken by a female-sounding voice (and lasts 1:12), while the second part (1:05) is delivered by a male-sounding voice whose aural qualities and content uncannily recall the Reapers, bio-technological creatures from deep space and deep time that embody mass extinction in the *Mass Effect* videogame trilogy (BioWare, 2007–2012). "The Unerasable Past" (2:50) features a less distorted voice delivering data about environmental destruction, accompanied by a melodic composition and a clean-vocals verse at the end: "And I count the days / 'Til we expire our ways. / And I count the days / 'Til we expire for always."

The remaining tracks are characterized by the apocalyptic imagery that defines the album. Thus, the lyrics exploit a variety of terms related to apocalyptic discourse and finitude (purge, extermination, extinction, euthanasia, demise, destruction, extinguished, poisoning, cremation, self-destructing power, sterilizing), negatively connotated verbs (infuriate, berate, subjugate, enrage, scavenge) and collocations (beyond compare, beyond repair, the scale has tipped, out of time, out of mind), and emphatic modifiers (inappropriate, hapless, ghastly, deep aggression, taunting). The album's pivotal argument is the protracted neglect that humanity has shown for the consequences of the exploitation, disregard, and pollution of the planet it has caused ("We know that we're wrong. / We know what we've done, / Yet we still carry on" ["Time's Cruel Curtain"]), for which "[w]e deserve everything that's coming" ("Death Atlas"). *Death Atlas* exposes the fact that environmental destruction and climate change affect the livelihoods of humans as well, but that does not seem to be a sufficient reason to mitigate any further damage because "profits dominate what's right" ("Vulturous"). The verses include constructions typical of radicalized misanthropic discourse, invoking the extinction of the human species ("Annihilation is necessary" ["The Great Dying II"]) while mourning the lives and species that anthropogenic activities have been exterminating.

The radically sounding lyrics suffer from their disconnect from the architectonics of environmental discourses and realpolitik. Radical environmentalism often brings forth conflicting notions and abstract solutions, failing to address underlying questions related to existing hegemonies. Furthermore, the dilemmas intrinsic to the construction of hierarchies in dealing with extinction and ecologies that are other situate such discourse "in pertinent existential questions that are culture-specific and need addressing as a prerequisite of working towards future global action in line with intercultural environmentalism" (Molek-Kozakowska 719). *Death Atlas* fails to propose any suggestions for solutions to the environmental crisis (other than ridding the planet of humankind) and remains trapped in a Western epistemology of extinction and climate change, overlooking the ecological crises that diverse populations on Earth have been facing. Indeed, this disregard for non-Western lifeworlds is a serious oversight because "the Anthropocene has reversed the temporal order of modernity: those at the margins are now the first to experience the future that awaits all of us" (Ghosh 62–63).

The arguments underpinning the lyrics do not advocate any kind of activism and do not speak up for mobilization. According to vocalist Travis Ryan, calling on people to blow up a pipeline (to draw on the title of Andreas Malm's recent book) is not the point, though: "We only produce questions, complaints, criticisms and problems" (quoted in Masters and Currin para 20). However, the lyrics arguably even fail to raise ecological awareness, as the references to environmental destruction become engulfed by the apocalyptic narrative that drives the album. As a result, the band's treatment of Anthropocene-related issues is a performance of a radical environmentalism that is mostly structured through discursive constructions and semantic choices, as well as perfunctory references to teleological, biblical, and mythical tropes (e.g., "We're flying too close to the sun" in "Absolute Destitute").

BRING BACK THE PLAGUE: ABSTRACT VS. CONCRETE PANDEMIC DISCOURSES

"Bring Back the Plague" is the seventh track of *Death Atlas*, following "One Day Closer to the End of the World," in which the lyrics express a "desire for the end times," decry human activities, and proclaim a "Lust for dying / Lust for extinction / Lusting for euthanasia." "Bring Back the Plague" continues along these lines by introducing the idea of a pandemic as a possible "solution" to humankind's cancerous existence on Earth (to draw on Cattle Decapitation's earlier song "Everyone Deserves to Die" [2002]). The lyrics of "Bring Back the Plague" exploit tropes typical of the "outbreak narrative" (Wald) and open with a direct reference to the Yersinia pestis bacterium. The use of the term "Black Death" not only generically refers to popular imaginations of outbreaks but also evokes the devastating scale of the bubonic plague wave in the fourteenth century, which wiped out about half the European population (Aberth 3). Aligned with their overall approach to extinction-related topics, Cattle Decapitation's treatment of the plague is driven more by a fascination with the decimation of humans and possible disruptions in the capitalist machinery than insight into plausible epidemiological developments.

By mentioning "[t]he recurring pandemic," the first verse evokes the "next pandemic" discourse. This discourse arose "in the early 1990s out of a shift in epidemiological reasoning, which ushered in the now prevalent notion of emerging infectious diseases" and refers to the notion of an upcoming pandemic event that will threaten the existence of humanity (Lynteris 6). Such discourse feeds the cyclical quality of what could be called the next-pandemic chronotope: human existence is bound to the expectation and unfolding of the next pandemic, in particular the spreading of zoonotic diseases, on a global, seemingly uncontainable scale. Despite the temporally linear irreversibility of the apocalyptic rhetoric, the chronotope relies on the idea of cyclically waiting for the eventual outbreak that will result in the end of the human species. As Déborah Danowski and Eduardo Viveiros de Castro underline, the next pandemic scenario is typically imagined as leading to a "world without us" rather than to "us without the world" (21). However, in *Death Atlas*, eschaton (or end of time, specifically for the human species) and katechon (time of the end, perceived as impending and caused by humanity itself) generally overlap.

Despite the exploitation of other common pandemic-related tropes and discursive constructions, the lyrics do not figure the "plague" as a malicious agent. When referring to pandemic events, such as COVID-19, the most common discursive construction of relatively new pathogens imagines them as somehow mysterious, elusive, and treacherous, characterized by an anthropomorphized sense of agency and prone to go undetected until their existence is revealed in fast-spreading outbreaks. For example, the bacterium of Yersinia pestis was long "believed to be able to escape detection and eradication by means of an array of strategies" (Lynteris 34). However, in "Bring Back the Plague," the virus assumes the role of an agent of justice, as the plague is personified as a mythical entity identified as "Black Death," who comes to "find us" and whose "cloak" is bound to "surround us" and actively exterminate humanity by "drown[ing] us / In bacillus countless." Despite this mythical, super-human dimension and its human-killing characteristics, the virus's anthropomorphism suggests that humankind is both the disease and its solution.

In terms of cultural history, the connection between the experience and knowledge of epidemiological events and the notion of human extinction is a relatively recent phenomenon. As Christos Lynteris observes, scientific literature only started exploring this concept in the 1990s, leading to the notion of humanity as faced "with a formidable microbiological agency that is asymmetrically more pervasive, elusive, virulent, or 'viral' (in terms of the communicative doxa of late capitalism) than humans" (36). The guiding metaphor of *Death Atlas* is that humanity is itself a virus that feeds not only on Earth's resources but also on its own livelihood, making the recurring and expected pandemic events the material consequence of such metaphorical infection and "diseased existence." Among the few references to epidemiological tropes, the lyrics use the image of "scattering rats" metaphorically to identify the human population prone to being infected and, at the same time, spreading the infection.

Rather than addressing questions such as taking preventive measures and/or preparing for the next pandemic, the lyrics of "Bring Back the Plague" identify the stark reduction of the number of humans inhabiting the planet as a desirable outcome; so much so that pandemics do not happen "often enough it seems." The vocals emphasize the importance of "find[ing] a way to rid the world of everyone tomorrow" and stress the purportedly democratic nature of infectious diseases, as "Every body [is] a host / Every body [can be] infected." However, the realities of the COVID-19 pandemic have demonstrated that a virus is not "the great equalizer," but rather exacerbates existing social inequalities (see, for example, Galasso; Mein).

In addition, the potentially equalizing human universalism imagined in the lyrics is riddled with inconsistencies. At the beginning of the song, the lyrics articulate a point of view that is external to the imagined pandemic event. The verses refer to a "populace" that is destined to become "a plague focus," delivering a generically misanthropic discourse. Further on, though, the lyrics refer to "us" as the target of the plague and invoke the extermination of "those that threaten a new world." This construction draws on the American apocalyptic tradition, which differentiates between sinners, who will be extinguished, and believers, who will populate the new world (see, for example, Zamora). In "Bring Back the Plague," this generic setup implies a hierarchy based on which some humans deserve infection and consequent annihilation more than others. That the lyrics do not specify who "those" who "threaten a new world" are results from the abstract quality of Cattle Decapitation's radical environmentalist discourse.

At the same time, the song exploits the dichotomic opposition between "us" and "them" typically employed in populist discourse. This construct seeks to create distance between the speaker and an antagonistic other that is entirely responsible for the negative acts at hand (van Dijk), which clashes with the album's underlying argument that humanity as a whole has contributed to the environmental disaster. Whereas most songs on the album employ the first-person plural to evoke species-thinking, "Bring Back the Plague" and "With All Disrespect" repeatedly use the second person. While the latter song deploys the pronoun to accuse an environmentally culpable yet nondescript "you," the former's use of the pronoun is key to the lyrics' ambiguousness. On the one hand, "you" refers directly to the virus and the pandemic: "Black Death, you've found us / Your cloak surrounds us." On the other hand, it refers to an interlocutor who "bring[s] back the plague" and who slowly becomes included in the mass of people deserving of extinction due to having ravaged the planet:

> Delete *those that threaten* a new world ...
>
> Dig *their* graves ...
>
> Bring back the plague
>
> Even if it means your own survival is at
> stake
>
> Dig *your* grave.
>
> We'll find a way to *rid the world of everyone*
> tomorrow ...
>
> Dig *our* grave. (our emphases)

The song thus suggests a responsibility for the environmental crisis shared among all of humankind and the inevitable outcome of anthropogenic activities that is extinction. Crucially, the lyrics do not indicate any type of solidarity among humans nor do they appeal to social responsibility. The music video, however, alters the perception of the lyrics.

REAL-LIFE PANDEMICS: THE MUSIC VIDEO

The "Bring Back the Plague" official music video opens with a distorted fragment of an official speech that Canadian prime minister Justin Trudeau delivered on March 23, 2020: "We've all seen the pictures online of people who seem to think they're invincible. Well, you're not. Enough is enough. Go home and stay home." The passage formed part of the opening of the speech, in which Trudeau condemned negationist attitudes and called upon Canadians to respect social distancing measures. The liberal prime minister punctuated his speech with harsh remarks to insist on the necessity for everyone to "do their part," while reassuring the population by pointing out the government's plans to cope with the virus and thanking essential workers (Trudeau). At that time, U.S. President Donald J. Trump repeatedly stressed the foreign (and specifically Chinese) origin of the virus, stated that his nondescript coronavirus team was "the best anywhere in the world" and claimed that the health risk for the majority of Americans was "very, very low" (Trump). The combination of downplaying the threat and glorifying the United States' opposition to the foreign otherness of the virus marked Trump's discursive approach to the pandemic and contributed to polarizing the electorate's positions. By integrating a meaningful fragment of Trudeau's speech into the music video, Cattle Decapitation signals a political position, distancing themselves from the U.S. presidential attitude.

After this introduction, the video shows different lockdown

practices and contexts that were experienced by subjects both situated inside their houses and venturing outside to provide for their livelihoods. The only epidemiological and plague-related trope used is a short clip showing a dead rat lying on a roadway, but the video avoids any further reference to zoonotic spread. Likewise, the foreign origin of the virus is only briefly hinted at when a cursor moves from China to the United States on a world map. Overall, the music video is deeply embedded in the coronavirus context to the point that for anyone unaware of what happened during the first few weeks of the coronavirus pandemic, the assembled clips would arguably be devoid of meaning.

Directly connected to real-life political discourse and concrete space-time, a new chronotopic dialogism of the (ongoing) pandemic emerges. The "inside" lockdown chronotope is marked by a familiar, circumscribed, and seemingly inescapable space, whereas time becomes an undefined parameter depending on the subject's perception influenced by the constant influx of news on pandemic developments. The impossibility to go outside and perform habitual tasks deconstructs time and binds it to the virtual, mediated connection with the outer world. The "outside" lockdown reality is equally marked by concrete locations that become the theater of narratives of quasi-ordeal, as people leave the "inside" chronotope to face a space and time that used to be familiar but has turned into an inhospitable and surreal version of reality.

This surreality is connected to how the pandemic—and in particular the first, unexpected lockdown—"distorts ordinary understandings of time by closing the geographical perimeters of public space" (Kattaga 1402). Chronological time, or *kronos*, was disrupted while the duration of mundane, everyday life, *kairos*, which is related to the unexpected but also to seizing moments, expanded (Hartog). Similar to how the Anthropocene suggests finitude with respect to life, the pandemic entails the idea of an ending—of "normalcy" but also possibly of humanity. It represents a temporal caesura and suggests a temporal order that transcends human existence by evoking a kind of posthuman time defined by "living with the virus."

As the coronavirus spread across the globe, in a very short period of time people were exposed to three new temporalities: the virus's own unknown temporal existence, the time imposed by the reaction to the spread through research and measures, and the time of the lockdown that coincided with a suspension of *chronos*. Avishek Parui and Merin Simi Raj have noted that a COVID-19-related crisis chronotope emerged from the uncertainty and defamiliarization of space-time intrinsic to the pandemic, leading to "a remapped engagement with materiality" (1434). In the configuration of a chronotope, space "becomes charged and responsive to the movements of time, plot and history," as time "thickens" (Bakhtin 84), becoming palpable and connected to a specific space. In the case of the consequences derived from the abrupt lockdown measures taken at the onset of the COVID-19 pandemic, a chronotopic ambivalence emerged from the clash between "compressed spatiotemporal connectedness and existential disconnect, whereby subjects share an infected time and space which also necessitates a distance which is defined as a social norm, avoidance of touch and only partially visible self" (Parui and Simi Raj 1435).

In an attempt to evidence the character of the pandemic as a social event and the uselessness of xenophobic "ground zero claiming," medical anthropologist A. David Napier has stressed that viruses are "just information waiting for a host." Such simplification resonates with the lyrics of "Bring Back the Plague," in which the concept of "host" is a focal point. However, the music video almost exclusively tackles the chronotopicity of early pandemic measures, focusing on the social consequences rather than the viral outbreak, condemning specific reactions and highlighting the pervasive disorientation generated by the sudden lockdowns. The music video's montage exposes how pandemic outbreaks are, in fact, "as much socially as biologically driven, being moments when information—for whatever reason—is socially shared, amplified, consumed, distorted, recycled and so on" (Napier). The awareness of the concreteness of disease and proximity of death is very likely to induce a "social meltdown" and "widespread disregard for law and custom …, and the public display of indulgence" (Lynteris 28).

The music video alternates between short fragments that are structured around two chronotopic dimensions. The "outside" pandemic experience is conveyed through clips showing people's aggressive reactions to imposed measures (Illustration 1), as well as people not following any guidance and instead traveling to Florida for spring break. Conversely, the "inside" space-time is connected to both a pandemic reinterpretation of images typical of music videos (showing the band members playing the song in their homes) and the visual commentary provided by the vocalist, Travis Ryan. Scenes in which Ryan appears tie the rather loosely assembled clips together, as his body language satirically comments on the imposed lockdown and on the absurdity of both the violence and the obliviousness displayed by people outside. The transition to "inside" clips is repeatedly characterized by a visual effect of static distortion, suggesting the presence of security cameras filming Ryan and the other band members, which touches upon the theme of surveillance evoked by lockdown measures. Besides generic stock footage of handwashing, wearing masks, blowing one's nose, and animations used to visualize the SARS-CoV-2 virus, a purposely placed clip shows a toilet paper roll descending a staircase, from the inside to the outside and from up down, thereby bridging the two chronotopic realities. The "outside" chronotope is characterized by signs of a possible social meltdown, revealed via social media clip: people panic-buy toilet paper and fight over goods and groceries, coping with the shortage that hit stores in the early stages of the pandemic.

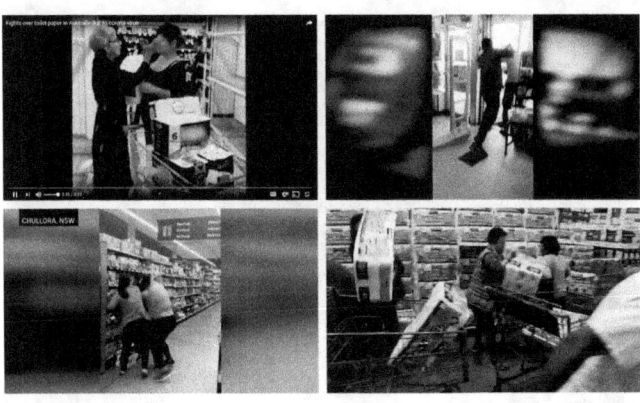

Illustration 1: The hunt for toilet paper leads to altercations.

With just a few clips sampled from video platforms, the images document the onset of anomic behaviors in the context of a pandemic event. The selection of clips supports the concept at the heart of the song: humans are the "virus"—in two senses: metaphorically by facilitating their own extinction with their (anti)social and individualistic behaviors and literally by thus spreading the virus. In a way, reality validated the notion underlying *Death Atlas* that humans often react in antisocial ways that amplify the damage already caused. A few clips showing people praying superposed with images of toilet paper rolls establish a link between the absurdity of herd behavior and (unmasked) mass prayers as a solution to a pandemic (Illustration 2). In other words, the music video satirizes how quickly people in the Global North idolized toilet paper and effectively turned it into the most prized commodity in the first few weeks of the coronavirus pandemic. At the same time, the images of worship critique people's misbegotten belief in religious practices as a "solution" to the viral spread instead of adhering to the guidelines published by the authorities.

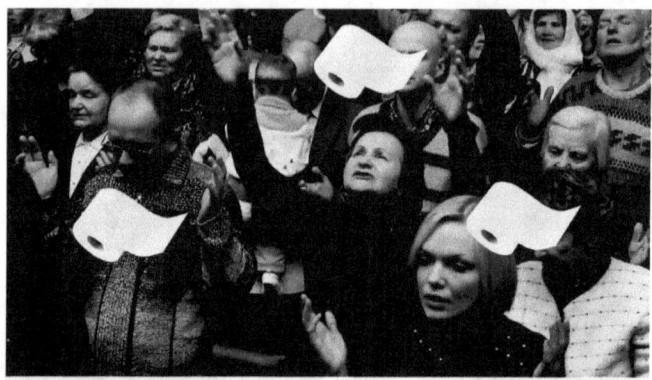

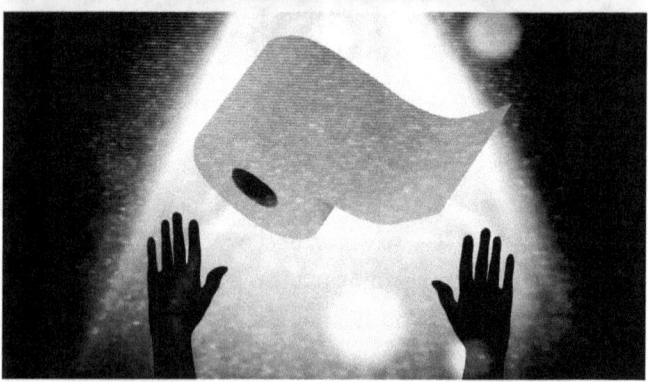

Illustration 2: Toilet paper assumes a divine quality.

Furthermore, the music video repeatedly includes footage of people spending time on beaches during spring break, especially young women dancing in swimsuits and entertained onlookers (Illustration 3). In the initial phase of the pandemic, the downplaying of viral spread within the United States led to the ban of foreign passengers from entering U.S. territory but did not regulate American citizens' travel. The lack of travel restrictions allowed students to spend their break on American and Mexican coasts; at the end of March, non-essential travel between the neighboring countries was only limited at land ports of entry (US CBP) and individuals assumed to be undocumented migrants (US CDC). Early college spring break (March 14–19, 2020) significantly increased viral spread in communities in which students had returned from popular destinations (e.g., Mandrum and Niekampt). The montage of Cattle Decapitation's video identifies spring breakers as a symbol of the super-spreader figure, as well as the embodiment of the lack of social responsibility and reckless attitudes that later were advocated by opponents of the pandemic measures imposed by the government. The reality of the pandemic depicted in the video confirms and expresses in a more concrete way Cattle Decapitation's consolidated criticism towards widespread individualism. The behaviors displayed in the clips expose a lack of social trust and the attendant inability to coordinate citizens' actions "in ways that are uncomfortable, inconvenient, and even painful to individuals, but crucial to collective well-being" (Napier and Fischer 275).

In the series of clips almost nobody is shown wearing masks except the band members, who are self-isolated in their homes: bassist Olivier Pinard and guitar players Josh Elmore and Belisario Dimuzio all wear different kinds of industrial safety masks and appear to be playing in their living rooms, while drummer Dave McGraw wears latex gloves, and vocalist Travis Ryan compulsively uses hand sanitizer (Illustration 4).

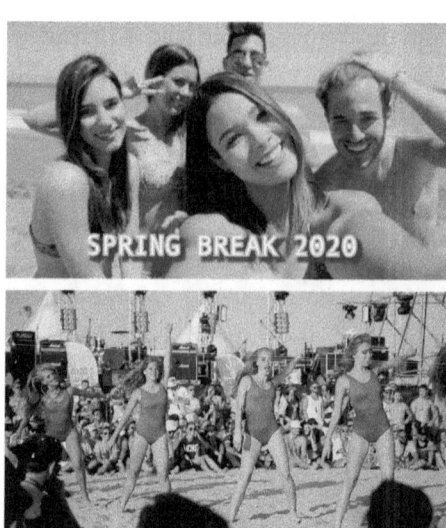

Illustration 3: Spring break helps spread the virus.

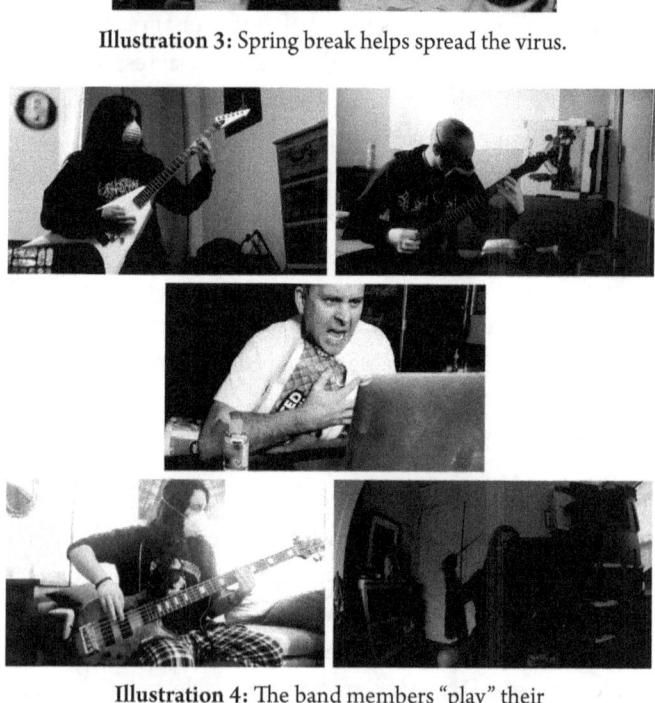

Illustration 4: The band members "play" their
instruments physically distanced from each other.

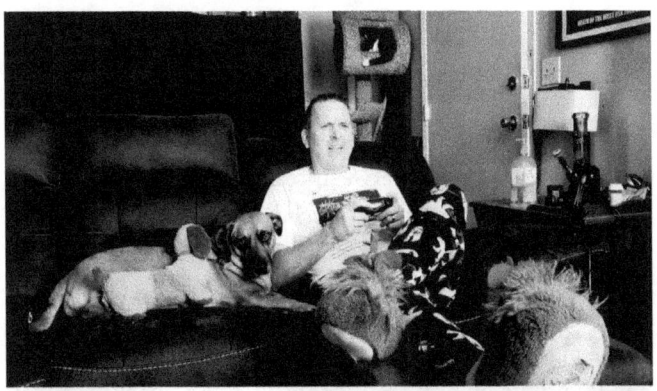

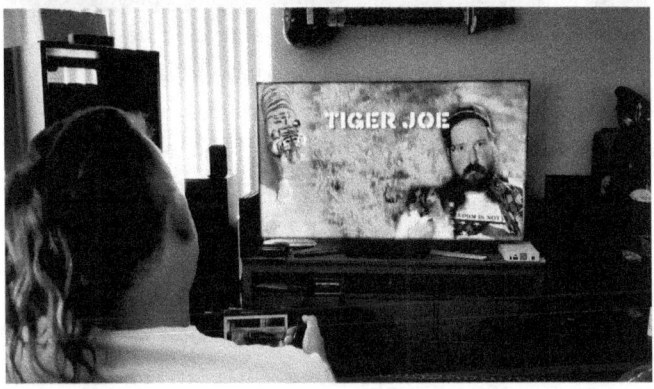

Illustration 5: Vocalist Travis Ryan plays videogames
and gives in to the media flow.

The "inside" chronotope is mostly detailed by clips featuring
the frontman, who expresses boredom, cynically observes
the unfolding events, and becomes frustrated by the (mis-)
information spread through the media. Partly owing to not
being able to work—which was especially relevant for musicians during the early stages of the pandemic—and the
limited array of activities available due to the sudden implementation of stay-at-home measures, Ryan seems to aban-
don himself to the passive exposure to all sorts of footage,
news, and television programs (Illustration 5). Coupling a

reference to popular culture with criticism of the kinds of content that were trending at the time, the music video briefly features a parody of Netflix's reality television show *Tiger King* (released on March 20, 2020). The fragment amplifies the perceived overlap between reality television shows and the "outside" chronotope, blurring the divide between fiction and reality, between misinformation and factual data on the pandemic.

Watching the news, the vocalist obsessively sanitizes his hands and the objects around him, hugging a package of toilet paper rolls while rocking in his sofa, as if he were stimming to cope with the coverage. His mood changes cyclically throughout the video, as he expresses disbelief, frustration, boredom, and apathy (Illustration 6). The lockdown activities he engages in manifest the domestic context, and yet they seem to get repetitive and eventually dull. Besides watching television and browsing the internet for information, Ryan plays video games and cuddles his pets in his living room, surrounded by personal belongings that represent his life, such as a bong, furry slippers, and a sitar. His condemnation of the irresponsible and anomic behaviors he witnesses and has access to from home is made clear through his reactions to the clips that viewers can see.

The music video thus removes the lyrics from their uncannily anticipatory-yet-nondescript timespace and transports them to the early days of the coronavirus pandemic in the United States, documenting this particular point in history as perceived and experienced by a large part of the general public. The video interweaves the experience of the inside chronotope, defined by increasing boredom, with an outside chronotope characterized by chaos. Uploaded in early April 2020, the music video originally conveyed a sense of liveness, as people across the Global North identified with the experiences represented, with YouTube user Evangelium, for example, remarking, "This is what we all needed during this time," while, for example, Jeff Buskirk pointed out the "clips from the crazy people in our society, and the massive hoarding and insane actions they are taking." Today, the music video still conveys this aura of past liveness, a memento of the onset of the pandemic.

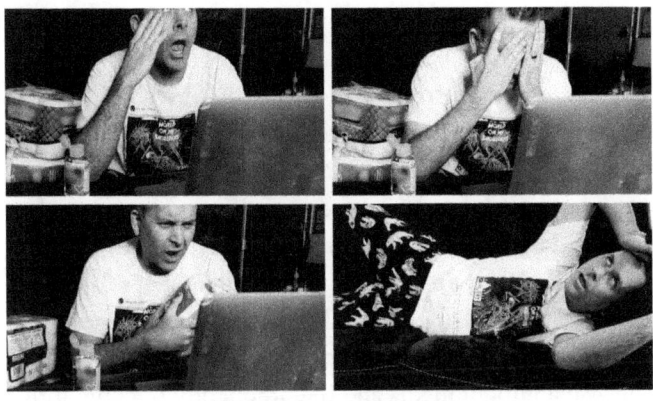

Illustration 6: Vocalist Travis Ryan going through the motions.

LOCKDOWN AND THE ARTIST

An insert in the music video highlights that "Bring Back the Plague" was filmed "on cell phones in self-isolation during the Covid 19 pandemic of March 2020." Resorting to a homemade mode of media production focusing on how they cope with the lockdown, Cattle Decapitation participated in the expression of agency that people with access to social media "had in shaping and sharing their experience of lonely isolation" (Redmond 186). The montage of low-tech clips and the appeal to a shared experience of the pandemic that revolves around the initial shock and difficulty to cope with stay-at-home measures is in line with a type of social media content that plays with notions of authenticity and personal disclosure. The construction of "an authentic self-representation can be understood as a way of telling the truth—about themselves" (García Santamaría 30) and, in this case, of revealing both the reality behind the artistic personae and the band's take on the social dimensions of the pandemic.

The depiction of the involuntary isolation that the band members were subjected to appeals to an idea of authenticity precisely because it is shared publicly on social media. This sharing of personal pandemic experiences through the music video resonates with how "ordinary people used the media to share their own stories of overcoming pandemic loneliness" (Redmond 185). The band's lockdown looks like the confinement ordinary people experienced in that moment, characterized by confusion, fear, and concern about the pandemic, as well as the boredom of unexpected forced isolation.[4] If, on the one hand, the start of the pandemic led to the abrupt cancellation of live concerts and tours, on the other hand, the availability of media and the production of content that tried to mediate the pandemic experience "has deepened the attachment to video and audio access to music at home. High-fidelity seems less important" (Botstein 353). Given the lack of live events and the concomitant necessity to move most daily activities online, "social media became filled with music videos and songs that related to the lockdown" (Alvarez-Cueva 6), eliciting a sense of solidarity and unity in view of the dramatic consequences of the viral spread.

In the "Bring Back the Plague" music video, such a function is

---

4   The band members' abodes (which are barely seen) also resemble ordinary people's homes, unlike, for example, Jimmy Fallon's house in the Hamptons, where he recorded the "Home Editions" of his late-night show.

present, albeit only subtly: the band participated in the public social discourse on COVID-19 by both engaging with the unexpected boredom of isolation and exposing the inability to dedicate themselves to their work. Despite the frustration with the situation depicted, the condemnation of selfish diversion and neglect of basic civility is clear and identified as a deviation from the solidarity among the American population that the authorities hoped to leverage. Similarly, *Death Atlas* diagnoses the lack of human solidarity with the nonhuman world and excoriates rugged individualism.

Nevertheless, there is an underlying conflict between the radical discourse typical of Cattle Decapitation's lyrics and their applicability to real-life events. Despite their misanthropic message, the band clearly engaged in the social event that the pandemic was from the get-go. Indeed, uploaded to YouTube, the music video exploits the platform, which "enables communities of shared interest to interact through words and images" (Strangelove 116). By being made publicly available and shareable, the music video was integrated into the practice of virtual-yet-social gatherings that came *en vogue* across the globe in early 2020, as Zoom's revenues skyrocketed. The fact that the band couldn't play together is made especially evident by the fact that the drummer had to resort to air-playing for the music video and reveals a sense of nostalgia brought about by the pandemic. Such feeling is subtly present in Cattle Decapitation's depiction of their coping mechanisms: the nostalgia for the ease of practicing together, which they enjoyed before the lockdown, is conveyed by the claustrophobic framing that their cell phones allow for, as well as the domestic environments characterized by disarray.

The stark contrast between the way the band members present themselves onstage and the middle-class domesticity that they represent in the video amplifies a sense of disruption and unreal disconnection from their pre-pandemic act. The abrupt change and the fear that nothing would "go back to normal" resulted in the creation and sharing of everyday pandemic experiences as a "[p]anic-stricken production of the real and of the referential" (Baudrillard 7). As Jean Baudrillard notes, when reality "is no longer what it was, nostalgia assumes its full meaning" (6). The social media exposure of ordinary coping with an extraordinary conjuncture thus becomes an "[e]scalation of the true, of lived experience, resurrection of the figurative" (Baudrillard 7), where real-life sociality was rendered impossible and "normal" activities disappeared. Such reaction and its depiction in the music video are limited to the lockdown experience lived by specific albeit ample strata of American society: essential workers did not enjoy the luxury of staying at home and kept on working throughout the pandemic, even in its early stages.

This neglect of the diversity of pandemic experiences and the attendant focus on the burden of staying at home for a few weeks—while ridiculing other people's ways to cope—ties into the different politics of the lyrics and (arguably tongue-in-cheek) music video of "Bring Back the Plague." The longing for the end of human existence expressed in the song's lyrics emerges from a very particular socio-cultural milieu in the Global North—a milieu that was quick to accept the large-scale restrictions on personal freedoms that COVID-19 and panic-stricken governments introduced to people's lives in spring 2020 (and a milieu that quickly whined about how difficult staying at home was). Similar to how governments around the world prioritized containing and "defeating" the coronavirus over climate actions, the music video's visuals and inserts—which locate "Bring Back the Plague" in the context of COVID-19 in the U.S.—overshadow the decidedly anti-humanist stance of the lyrics. Ultimately, the move from "eating / Humanity to nevermore" in the lyrics to "stay home" and "listen to Death Atlas" in a title card at the end of the music video demonstrates that once reality threatens to impinge upon the luxuries one has become accustomed to, one's ideals are quickly forgotten. In addition, the reference to buying *Death Atlas* (even if meant jokingly) suggests that what Naomi Klein has dubbed "disaster capitalism" also defines the lives of bands who purportedly oppose the ill-defined "system."

The inability to detach themselves from capitalism is encapsulated by the t-shirt Travis Ryan wears in the music video. The shirt remembers how rapper Teddy YG used the *Death Atlas* cover art (including the band's logo and all) for a mixtape he released a few weeks prior to Cattle Decapitation's album. The band quickly turned this theft into merchandise, selling a limited edition of the shirt in question, which shows an image of the rapper's Instagram post that made the copyright breach public, for twenty-four hours on October 10 and 11, 2019 (Cattle Decapitation, "YES, THIS IS REAL"). Typical of capitalist production processes, the work of artist Wes Benscoter was rarely (if ever) acknowledged in online discussions surrounding the incident, severing the connection between the actual creator and the final product in an attempt to capitalize on the environmental destruction of the planet.

To be sure, Cattle Decapitation's exploitation of the devastating anthropogenic impact on Earth's life systems does not bring them great financial profit; however, both the reference to buying *Death Atlas* at the end of the music video and the repeated references to transforming copyright breach into a commodity throughout the video seem to suggest that it may be "easier for us today to imagine the thoroughgoing deterioration of the earth and nature than the breakdown of late capitalism," to quote an overused phrase by Fredric Jameson (xii). Indeed, by clinging to this capitalist worldview, human activities focus on short-term questions, while the ecological crisis has been unfolding slowly. But from a capitalist point of view, these long-term developments do not really matter, for, to quote John Maynard Keynes out of context, "[*i*]*n the long run*, we are all dead," anyways (65).

Note: Michael Fuchs would like to thank the Volkswagen Foundation for funding received for the project Pandemic Meets Fiction

WORKS CITED

Aberth, John. "Introduction: The Black Death in History." The *Black Death: The Great Mortality of 1348–1350*, edited by John Aberth, Palgrave Macmillan, 2005, pp. 1–7.

Alvarez-Cueva, Priscila. "Music to Face the Lockdown: An Analysis of Covid-19 Music Narratives on Individual and Social Well-Being." *Social Inclusion*, vol. 10, no. 2, 2022, pp. 6–18.

Bakhtin, Mikhail Mikhailovich. *The Dialogic Imagination: Four Essays*. Translated by Caryl Emerson and Michael Holquist, U of Texas P, 1981.

Baudrillard, Jean. *Simulacra and Simulation*. Translated By Sheila Faria Glaser. U of Michigan P, 1994.

Bennett, Jane. *Vibrant Matter: A Political Ecology of Things*. Duke UP, 2010.

Botstein, Leon. "The Future of Music in America: The Challenge of the COVID-19 Pandemic." The *Musical Quarter-*

ly, no. 102, 2020, pp. 351–360.

Cattle Decapitation. "Cattle Decapitation - Bring Back the Plague (OFFICIAL VIDEO)." *YouTube,* uploaded by Metal Blade Records, 2 Apr. 2020, https://www.youtube.com/watch?v=lXGSLKWeVwE

Cattle Decapitation. *Death Atlas.* Metal Blade Records, 2019.

Cattle Decapitation. "Everyone Deserves to Die." *To Serve Man.* Metal Blade Records, 2002.

Cattle Decapitation. "YES, THIS IS FOR REAL!!" Twitter, 10 Oct. 2019, https://twitter.com/cattledecap/status/1182359796063686656.

Cragg, Michael. "Björk's *Biophilia*." *The Guardian,* 28 May 2011,www.theguardian.com/culture/2011/may/28/bj-rks-biophilia.

Danowski, Déborah, and Eduardo Viveiros de Castro. *The Ends of the World.* Polity, 2016.

Fagan, Madeleine. "Who's Afraid of the Ecological Apocalypse? Climate Change and the Production of the Ethical Subject." *The British Journal of Politics and International Relations,* vol. 19, no. 2, 2017, pp. 225–244.

Foucault, Michael. "A Preface to Transgression." *Language, Counter-Memory, Practice: Selected Essays and Interviews,* edited and translated by Donald F. Bouchard. Cornell UP, 1977, pp. 21–53.

Galasso, Vincenzo. "COVID: Not a Great Equalizer." *CESifo Economic Studies,* vol. 66, no. 4, 2020, pp. 376–393.

García Santamaría, Sara. "Politicians 'Stay Home': Left-Wing

Populism and Performances of the Intimate Self on So-
cial Media During the COVID-19 Pandemic." *Networking Knowledge*, vol. 14, no. 1, 2021, pp. 28–50.

Ghosh, Amitav. *The Great Derangement: Climate Change and the Unthinkable*. U of Chicago P, 2016.

Guðmundsdóttir, Björk, and Timothy Morton. "This Huge Sunlit Abyss from the Future Right There Next to You …: Emails between Björk Guðmundsdóttir and Timothy Morton," edited by James Merry. *Björk: Archives*. Museum of Modern Art, 2015, n. pag.

Hartog, François. *Chronos: L'Occident aux prises avec le Temps*. Gallimard, 2020.

Jameson, Fredric. *The Seeds of Time*. Columbia UP, 1996.

Kahn-Harris, Keith. *Extreme Metal: Music and Culture on the Edge*. Berg, 2007.

Kattago, Siobhan. 2021. "Ghostly Pasts and Postponed Fu-
tures: The Disorder of Time During the Corona Pandemic." *Memory Studies*, vol. 14, no. 6, 2021, pp. 1401–1413.

Keynes, John Maynard. *The Collected Writings of John Maynard Keynes, Vol. IV: A Tract on Monetary Reform*. 1923. Cambridge UP, 2013.

Kidner, David W. "Why 'Anthropocentrism' Is Not Anthropocentric." *Dialectical Anthropology*, no. 38, 2014, pp. 465–480.

Klein, Naomi. *The Shock Doctrine: The Rise of Disaster Capitalism*. Metropolitan Books, 2007.

Lynteris, Christos. *Human Extinction and the Pandemic Imag-*

inary. London: Routledge, 2020.

Malm, Andreas. *How to Blow Up a Pipeline: Learning to Fight in a World of Fire*. Verso, 2021.

Masters, Marc, and Grayson Currin. "Digging Back in The Out Door." *Pitchfork*, 22 June 2012, https://pitchfork.com/features/the-out-door/8870-digging-back-in/.

Mein, Stephen A. "COVID-19 and Health Disparities: The Reality of 'The Great Equalizer.'" *Journal of General Internal Medicine*, vol. 35, no. 8, 2020, pp. 2439–2440.

Molek-Kozakowska, Katarzyna. "Environmental Activism as Counter-Hegemony? A Critical Discourse Analysis of (Self)Representations of Radical Environmental Organizations Across Cultures." *Language and Intercultural Communication*, vol. 21, no. 6, 2021, pp. 717–733. https://doi.org/10.1080/14708477.2021.1979570

Morton, Timothy. *Dark Ecology: For a Logic of Future Coexistence*. Columbia UP, 2016.

Morton, Timothy. "Guest Column: Queer Ecology." *PMLA*, vol. 125, no. 2, 2010, pp. 273–282.

Morton, Timothy. "Subscendence." *e-flux*, no. 85, 2017, www.e-flux.com/journal/85/156375/subscendence/.

Morton, Timothy. "Thank Virus for Symbiosis." *STRP*, 4 Apr. 2020, strp.nl/updates/thank-virus-for-symbiosis.

Müller, Timo. "The Ecology of Literary Chronotopes." *Handbook of Ecocriticism and Cultural Ecology*, edited by Hubert Zapf, De Gruyter, 2016, pp. 590–604.

Napier, A. David. "No ground zero?" *Le Monde Diplomatique*.

March 7, 2022.

Napier, A. David, and Edward F. Fischer. "Misunderstanding a Viral Pandemic: The Social and Cultural Contexts of COVID-19." *Social Research: An International Quarterly*, vol. 87, no. 2, 2020, pp. 271–277.

Parui, Avishek, and Merin Simi Raj. "The COVID-19 Crisis Chronotope: The Pandemic as Matter, Metaphor and Memory." *Memory Studies*, vol. 14, no. 6, 2021, pp. 1431–1444. https://doi.org/10.1177/17506980211054346

Pratt, Mary Louise. "Coda: Concept and Chronotope." *Arts of Living on a Damaged Planet: Monsters of the Anthropocene*, edited by Anna Tsing et al., U of Minnesota P, 2017, pp. G169–G174.

Pratt, Mary Louise. *Planetary Longings*. Duke UP, 2022.

Redmond, Sean. "A Pandemic of Creative Loneliness." *Continuum: Journal of Media & Cultural Studies*, vol. 36, no. 2, 2022, pp. 184–198.

Rothe, Delf. "Governing the End Times? Planet Politics and the Secular Eschatology of the Anthropocene." *Millennium: Journal of International Studies*, vol. 48, no. 2, 2020, pp. 143–164.

Ryan, Travis. Interview with Jim Costin. *The Moshville Times*, 22 July 2015, https://www.moshville.co.uk/interview/2015/07/interview-travis-ryan-of-cattle-decapitation/.

Seymour, Nicole. *Bad Environmentalism: Irony and Irreverence in the Ecological Age*. U of Minnesota P, 2018.

Strangelove, Michael. *Watching YouTube: Extraordinary Videos by Ordinary People.* U of Toronto P, 2010.

Trudeau, Justin. Coronavirus News Briefing. 23 Mar. 2020, Ottawa, Canada.

Trump, Donald J. Coronavirus Pandemic Speech. 11 Mar. 2020, Washington D.C., USA.

U.S. Centers for Disease Control and Prevention. Order Suspending Introduction of Certain Persons from Countries Where a Communicable Disease Exists, under Sections 362 & 365 of the Public Health Service Act, (42 U.S.C. 265, 268), 20 Mar. 2020.

U.S. Customs and Border Protection. Notification of Temporary Travel Restrictions Applicable to Land Ports of Entry and Ferries Service Between the United States and Mexico, 24 Mar. 2020.

van Dijk, Teun A. "Discourse and manipulation." *Discourse and Society*, vol. 17, no. 3, 2006, pp. 359–383.

van Ooijen, Erik. "Giving Life Harmoniously: Animal Inversion in Cattle Decapitation." *Helvete: A Journal of Black Metal Theory*, no. 2, 2015, pp. 73–95.

Wald, Priscilla. *Contagious: Cultures, Carriers, and the Outbreak Narrative.* Duke UP, 2008.

Weheliye, Alexander G. *Habeas Viscus: Racializing Assemblages, Biopolitics, and Black Feminist Theories of the Human.* Duke UP, 2014.

Yusoff, Kathryn. *A Billion Black Anthropocenes or None.* U of Minnesota P, 2018.

Zamora, Lois Parkinson. *Writing the Apocalypse: Historical Vision in Contemporary U.S. and Latin American Fiction.* Cambridge UP, 1989.

Satirical Comedy Does COVID-19: John Oliver as Science Journalist

By Shelly Galliah

ABSTRACT

This article analyzes selected segments of John Oliver's *Last Week Tonight*, which were dedicated to conveying accurate COVID-19 information, debunking coronavirus falsehoods, addressing pandemic-related sociocultural issues, and exposing conspiracy theories. In these videos, John Oliver corrects the commercial press while adopting several science journalist roles: that of explainer, investigative, and civic educator journalists. Oliver's videos, whose reach extends far beyond his original audience, are valuable resources for conveying accurate information and teaching critical thinking.

Keywords: John Oliver, *Last Week Tonight*, satirical comedy, satire, science journalist, science journalism, explainer journalism, investigative journalism, Fox News, conspiracy theories

La comedia satírica hace COVID-19: John Oliver como periodista científico

RESUMEN

Este artículo analiza segmentos seleccionados de *Last Week Tonight* de John Oliver, que se dedicaron a transmitir información precisa sobre el COVID-19, desacreditar falsedades sobre el coronavirus, abordar problemas socioculturales relacionados con la pandemia y exponer teorías de conspiración. En estos videos, John Oliver corrige a la prensa comercial mientras adopta varios roles de periodista científico: el de periodista explicativo, de investigación y educador cívico. Los videos de Oliver, cuyo alcance se extiende mucho más allá de su audiencia original, son recursos valiosos para transmitir información precisa y enseñar el pensamiento crítico.

Palabras clave: John Oliver, *Last Week Tonight*, comedia satírica, sátira, periodista científico, periodismo científico, periodismo explicativo, periodismo de investigación, Fox News, teorías de la conspiración

讽刺喜剧聚焦2019冠状病毒病：约翰·奥利弗担任科学记者

摘要

本文分析了约翰·奥利弗（John Oliver）主持的《上周今夜秀》的部分视频，这些视频聚焦于传递准确的2019冠状病毒病（COVID-19）信息、揭穿关于冠状病毒的谎言、应对与大流行相关的社会文化问题、以及揭露阴谋论。在这些视频中，约翰·奥利弗纠正了商业媒体，同时担任了几个科学记者的角色：解释型记者、调查型记者和公民教育记者。奥利弗的视频影响范围远远超出了他的原始受众，并且这些视频是传递准确信息和教授批判性思维的宝贵资源。

关键词：约翰·奥利弗，《上周今夜秀》，讽刺喜剧，讽刺，科学记者，科学新闻学，解释新闻学，调查新闻学，福克斯新闻，阴谋论

On March 11, 2020, in a speech on the coronavirus outbreak, the Director-General of the World Health Organization (WHO) declared that "pandemic is not a word to use lightly or carelessly. It is a word that, if misused, can cause unreasonable fear, or unjustified acceptance that the fight is over, leading to unnecessary suffering and death." In the United States, both *pandemic* the word and *pandemic* the phenomenon would soon spark fear, uncertainty, acquiescence, anger, and political polarization—both about the severity of the coronavirus as well as the strategies for preventing it. Very shortly, in fact, there would be an infodemic characterized by various kinds of circulating untruths: misinformation, disinformation, and propaganda, which have different purposes. According to Benkler et al., disinformation is the intentional "dissemination of explicitly false or misleading information" often for political purposes (32), whereas misinformation is the de-politicized circulation of lies and fallacies, often from the result of bad facts and misunderstandings (24). Propaganda, on the other hand, is "designed to manipulate a target population by affecting its beliefs, attitudes, or preferences in order to obtain behavior compliant with [the] political goals of the propagandist" (29) or to create "controversy where none previously existed" in order to stall progress and undermine democracy (Rabin-Havt 6). These circulating untruths would soon permeate the mediasphere, creating an infodemic that confused already panicked publics.

Stepping in to respond to this infodemic was comedian and satirical commentator John Oliver. That is, between March 2020 and November 2020 (Season 7), and again in Season 8, Oliver dedicated several episodes of his program *Last Week Tonight* to communicating accurate coronavirus information, analyzing coronavirus-related issues, and debunking various types of incorrect information. These efforts were not the first time that Oliver used his program, for which he has full "creative freedom" (Guthrie) to expose issues and intervene on incorrect information. Almost immediately after launching *Last Week Tonight*, Oliver tackled controversial issues and stories underplayed by other news outlets, such as the General Motors' ignition recall, the tax-free status of churches, food waste, unethical election policies, and backwards American sex education. He also enlivened dry, but confusing technological subjects (debt-buying, Bitcoin, multi-level marketing, and net neutrality); and informed viewers about complicated global issues ignored by traditional news programs (the growth of authoritarian leaders and the threat of Vladimir Putin).

Despite Oliver's satirical approach, various award-granting agencies began recognizing his work on *Last Week Tonight* as journalism. In his first Peabody Award (for the original net neutrality segment), Jeffrey Jones commended Oliver for his "resolve not simply to explore headline news, but to pull back the proverbial curtain and show us the subtle mechanics at work in our nation's democracy and culture . . . For bringing satire and journalism even closer together." Soon after, online writers, such as Suebsang and Poniezowik, began qualifying Oliver's method as investigative journalism as well as explainer journalism, which, according to Zhang, summarizes complex stories or dry technical topics, unpacks key terms, and deconstructs any spin, so that readers/viewers may best understand future developments. Some, such as Victor Luckerson, also began speaking of the John Oliver effect: the comedian's talent of setting the news agenda and drawing renewed attention to an underplayed or forgotten issue, often sparking public outrage and then action. The earliest example of the Oliver effect was the conclusion of his June 1, 2014, segment on preserving net neutrality. Alarmed that the FCC was not taking this matter seriously, Oliver urged his viewers to go to the internet and focus their "indiscriminate rage in a useful direction." "Seize your moment, my lovely trolls, turn on caps lock, and fly my pretties! Fly! Fly!" Viewers responded by flooding the usually underused (and buried) FCC website with 45,000 comments, slowing it to a crawl. Eventually, Kastrenakes notes, the FCC received 3.7 million comments on net neutrality. This video, which still attracts attention with over 16 million YouTube views, demonstrates the longevity and virality of Oliver's satirical messaging.

Along with commenting on current affairs, Oliver and other late-night hosts have dedicated considerable time and effort to discussing scientific topics and their related sociocultural and political issues. The author's previous research noted how Seth Myers, Jon Stewart, Stephen Colbert, Samantha Bee, and Jimmy Kimmel have all addressed contentious scientific topics, such as the climate change crisis, distrust in scientific authority, and vaccine hesitancy. And media critics have taken notice of their efforts, too, analyzing the affordances and constraints of late-night celebrities delivering science news. Feldman and Young, for instance, have weighed in on how satirical television programs, such as *Last Week Tonight*, *The Daily Show*, *The Colbert Report*, which have more latitude than the legacy press in selecting and covering issues, often explain complex scientific topics and by, extension, improve scientific literacy (2008). Instead of 30-second soundbites wedged between more important stories, hosts of these programs can aggregate rich content about the sociocultural issues affecting science; they responsibly represent complicated scientific subjects (climate change, the GMO controversy) without falling into the journalistic trap of balance as bias. And satirical comedy has the advantage of getting people watching and listening; that is, Brewer and McKnight contend that the comedic affordances of these programs—frequent jokes, a sarcastic tone, ample popular culture references—may reinvigorate stale subject matter and draw previously detached viewers to scientific subjects (651). This writer, for instance, has used satirical comedy as a pedagogical resource for depicting the logical fallacies associated with vaccine hesitancy.

The efforts of these late-night hosts are but one example of the transformation of the science journalism mediasphere;[1] that is, there has been a dramatic expansion online in both participatory science reporting and accommodated online science-related information (tweets, blogs, social media, popular science websites). According to science journalism scholar Trench, these trends have created an "overlapping information and communication space" in which audiences can receive scientific content from various online contributors and in both formal and informal ways (cited in Nisbet "Online"). Recognizing these changes, many science historians have expanded the definition of science journalism to include all news "related to science in the broadest sense of the word, including, but not limited to science as a process, scientific findings, science institutions (or individuals), and encompassing all kinds of science, including humanities and

---

1 "Applying this idea, the evolving science media ecosystem consists of legacy media in their print and online formats, including the *Guardian* and the *New York Times*; science blogging and aggregation sites, most notably Scienceblogs.com; the news and blogging communities formed by journals such as *Science, Nature* and *PLoS*; the news and blogging communities formed by legacy science magazines including *Discover* and *Scientific American*; ideologically-driven advocacy blogs and sites such as *Pharyngula, Climate Progress* and *Climate Depot*; and reflexive and meta-discussions of science journalism at MIT's *Knight Science Journalism Tracker* and the *Colombia Journalism Review*."

natural sciences" (Korthagen and Wormer, cited in Bos and Nuigens 121). These changes have been accompanied by a reduction of science journalists in legacy media outlets and the creation of different kinds of scientific authority. Late-night comedy and satirical programs, because of their significant viewers and virality, should also be added to this list of viable science journalism sources.

In the changing online media ecosystem, science reporters have adapted by taking on different professional roles and routines. To categorize these, Nisbet interviewed several science journalism professionals—those from legacy news outlets, popular science magazines, journals, and online science mags, and one science book writer. He classified their roles as conduits, information curators, civic educators, public intellectuals, agenda-setters, watchdogs, and conveners. In Nisbet's interview, only a few identified as civic educators or agenda setters. Some envisioned themselves as watchdogs, standing over and critically evaluating "scientific institutions and the scientific community, but also over individuals or groups making false scientific claims, and over social actors intervening in science policy discussions"; and as conveners, who connect scientists with their publics to discuss science. However, the majority of those interviewed considered their main roles to be conduits, curators, and public intellectuals. As conduit or explainer journalist, one's job is summarizing and explaining science understandably to non-specialists. Second to this role is that of the curator, who aggregates science-related content to evaluate it so that publics can make informed opinions. This role also encompasses teaching others about the scientific process. Those interviewed said they sometimes adopt the role of public intellectuals, which is similar to traditional newspaper commentators or columnists; they present topics from their specific worldview. Public intellectuals also function as critical debunkers, calling out exaggerated or false claims about science. In taking on these roles, journalists aim to improve scientific literacy, the understanding of the scientific process, and trust in scientific authority.

Oliver has previously adopted these science journalism roles in *Last Week Tonight*. For instance, acting as conduit and aggregator, Oliver has dissected and collected sources about scientific and technical topics ignored and/or misinterpreted by the commercial press: nuclear waste management, forensic evidence, CRISPR, sexism and racism in medicine, the accommodation of scientific articles, and the regulation of compounding pharmacies. Taking on the public intellectual role, he has also exposed manufactroversies—those science issues that are "manufactured in the public sphere when an arguer announces that there is an ongoing scientific debate in the technical sphere about a matter for which there is actually an overwhelming scientific consensus on the corresponding issue" (Ceccarelli 269). Oliver's earliest dismantling of a manufactroversy was his 2014 "Statistically Representative Climate Change Debate," which was lauded by several (Fung; Galliah; Mooney; Nuticelli) for its clear visual representation of false balance. (Oliver has also addressed the spurious connection between vaccines and autism; the lack of safety of genetically modified foods; and the Paris Agreement as a global plot against American interests.)

Science communicators, regardless of their role, also regularly draw attention to or use framing devices, which according to Cormack are one of the most important tools (100). Drawing upon Goffman, Lakoff describes frames as mental schema or structures that "shape the way we see the world. As a result, they shape the goals we seek, the plans we make, the way we act, and what counts as a good or bad outcome of our actions. In politics our frames shape our social policies and the institutions we form to carry out policies" (1-2). Or to put it another way, frames are "the interpretive storylines that set a specific train of thought in motion, communicating about how an issue might be a problem, who or what is responsible for it, and what should be done about it" (Nisbet, "Communicating" 15). Frames provided by the media often act as interpretive shortcuts or mental heuristics. Although frames determine what should be talked about and what questions can be asked, they are a "valence-neutral organizing device for audiences and interpretations" (Nisbet, "Framing" 45); that is, they may be used for pro-issue, anti-issue, and neutral positions. Nisbet, extended Gamson and Modigliani's original list, has summarized eight basic frames in communicating science policy issues: social progress; economic development /competitiveness; morality/ethics; scientific/technical uncertainty; Pandora's box/ Frankenstein's monster/runaway science; public accountability/governance; middle way/alternative path; and conflict/strategy ("Framing" 50-51). John Oliver is quite familiar with framing; in previous episodes, he has exposed how the framing of climate change in terms of both scientific uncertainty (the climate change debate is still open) and conflict (the economy versus the environment; the U.S. versus the world; and European elitism against American values) has warped the public's understanding of the climate crisis. In his 2015 segment on President Trump's "Paris Agreement," Oliver focused on the president's use of the conflict frame in depicting this agreement (the U.S. against the world), which allowed him to make base appeals to ethnocentrism, American exceptionalism, and fear.

Science journalism may have evolved, and the roles of science journalists may have changed, but the need for science

news is as important as ever. And in a pandemic characterized by misinformation and disinformation, accurate news
is even more crucial in informing publics and mitigating a
health crisis. In his coronavirus segments (see Table), which
ran between March 2020 and May 2021, Oliver stepped in to
confront the faulty coverage of the pandemic by the commercial press and by other less reputable news sources. In most
of these monologues, Oliver acts as a conduit science journalist, explaining the most recent coronavirus developments.
He summarizes the facts about the coronavirus and translates
(and supports) advice from relevant health officials. He also
takes on the role of information curator, collecting stories
about the coronavirus, in order to put them into perspective
and comment on them. As the series progresses and the comedian becomes more concerned about the pandemic and
vulnerable populations, his tone becomes more urgent and
he slides into the watchdog and public intellectual roles, dis-
tinguishing truths from falsehoods and debunking scientific
conspiracies. Secondly, in these coronavirus episodes, Oliver
not only adopts these journalistic roles but also draws attention to how the facts (or myths) about the coronavirus are
being framed. Additionally, he employs these frames himself
to persuade his audience of the coronavirus crisis and the importance of personal and public responsibility in preventing
the disease's spread. Due to the constraint of length, this paper
will focus only on Oliver's 2020 coronavirus episodes. It will
analyze a selection of those from the beginning of the crisis
(March 2020) to the first major spike in cases (July 2020).

OLIVER AS EXPLAINER SCIENCE JOURNALIST

Before an analysis of Oliver's journalistic roles, it is important
to say something about his method, which distinguishes his
work from that of other late-night hosts. Instead of including

short comic segments in his program, Oliver delivers long satirical monologues, which average around twenty minutes. Though his satirical monologues look effortless, they are crafted of four different components (Galliah): comic segments, satirical targets, snippets of information, and calls to action. In the comic segments, the glue holding the various pieces together, Oliver makes jokes (both low and high), states ridiculous comparisons, raises his voice, uses exaggerated gestures and bodily movements, and shows silly visuals. In the satirical components, Oliver aims his arrows at media coverage, media figures, political elites, events, fabrications, misrepresentations, and so on, which are then ridiculed and then corrected. It is in the other components of his monologues (snippets of information and calls to action) that Oliver drops his persona (mask) and earnestly takes on the roles of journalist and public intellectual concerned about delivering accurate news, correcting falsehoods, and informing his viewers. Oliver's monologues always consist of well-researched evidence drawn from very credible sources: government reports, newspaper and scientific articles, televised news segments, and experts. These sources are accompanied by both references and images so that audiences may then visualize and verify them, continuing their learning after the episode is done. Oliver often concludes his monologues with calls to action, such as imperatives to contact your local politician, donate to a cause, research a subject, or, simply, *think*.

In his first three coronavirus episodes, Oliver acts as conveyer journalist using several science communication strategies—frames, allusions, and analogies—to communicate his subject matter. His very first episode, "COVID-19 Pandemic and Governmental Response in the US" (7.3, March 11, 2020) offers an eerie snapshot into the innocuous beginnings of the coronavirus epidemic: the first dozen infections and the first death in the United States; 2700 deaths in China; the coronavirus in 60 countries. (At the time of this writing, according to *The New York Times* and Our World in Data, the number of cases in the United States is 93.9 million, whereas the death toll stands at 1.04 million.) Oliver's main objectives in this episode are communicating accurate coronavirus information while assuaging his audience's fears. Although he expresses deep concern about the coronavirus, overall, his mood is still positive, his monologue upbeat, and his jokes silly: allusions to *Sesame Street*, comments about dirty cruise ships, and jibes about Mike Pence. He announces that he wants to get "the very basics down here straight away" (1:49), which, for Oliver, is explaining the origin of the virus (deaths in China and the appearance of the coronavirus in 60 other European countries), defining virus statistics (the 2% mortality rate and the easy spread of the disease), critiquing China and Japan's original inept handling of the virus, and effusively praising Vietnam's effective hand-washing campaign. As for satire, his main target is a familiar one—the bungled information disseminated by the Trump administration. However, there is a greater sense of urgency now—the president's actions and inactions are a matter of life and death.

In his messaging, Oliver blends his satirical science communication with two frames: the Pandora's box frame and the public accountability and governance frame. The Pandora's box/Frankenstein monster/runaway science frame involves framing facts in terms of "a need for precaution or action in face of possible catastrophe and out-of-control consequences; or alternatively as fatalism, where there is no way to avoid the consequences or chosen path" (Nisbet, "Communicating" 18). In its positive valence, this frame motivates action on an issue; in its negative valence, it promotes fear, pessimism, and acquiescence—a sense that it is too late to stop the runaway train of catastrophe. Communicators often invoke the public accountability and governance frame when they discuss "research or policy either in the public interest or serving public interests [while] emphasizing issues of control, transparency, participation, responsiveness, or ownership; or debate over proper use of science and expertise in decision-making" (Nisbet, "Communicating" 18). When science journalists use this frame, they are focusing on how government officials are communicating about an issue transparently, handling scientific research accurately, guarding public interests, and using their leadership responsibly. This is also the frame used to politicize science issues for both positive and negative ends.

Right at the beginning of the episode, Oliver employs yet tempers the catastrophe frame. That is, in the segment's first 26 seconds, he flashes upsetting clips about the pandemic from several respected news sources (*World News Tonight, CBS, Good Morning America*). On the screen are disturbing images of people in Hazmat suits, frantic healthcare workers, and public panic while the hurried soundbites mention "global hot zones," "fears of coronavirus spreading," "spike in cases," and a "race to contain the outbreak." After aggregating these stories, Oliver stands over the news with this warning from the CDC: "It is not a matter of if, but when." However, almost immediately, he deflates this grim news by using two popular culture allusions demonstrating what "not if, but when" means—it is not a matter of "if, but when" Saoirse Ronan will win an Oscar and Henry Kissinger will die. (Henry Kissinger, at the age of 99, is currently ranked #2 on the celebrity death list.) Throughout his entire monologue, in fact, Oliver artfully balances disturbing COVID facts with jokes. For instance, after introducing the startling prediction that, in only one year, 40-70% of the world will be infected,

Oliver jokes that the only disease that should be infecting the world at that rate is "Adam Driver fever." And after relating how the Chinese government enforced the Wuhan lockdown by putting suitcase-sized speakers on sidewalks, Oliver says he much prefers the American nightmare of having small talking boxes in our homes and being told by Jeff Bezos to buy underwear. In short, throughout this episode, Oliver tries to keep his audience listening by keeping them laughing.

At the same time, Oliver assures his audience that the coronavirus pandemic *is a crisis* by invoking the catastrophe frame himself. First, he stresses the 2% mortality rate, a stat being (ab)used in certain media circles to demonstrate that fears about the coronavirus are exaggerated. At 2:37, Oliver targets both Chuck Todd's comments that COVID-19's 2% mortality rate is "not that bad" and social media is depicting the virus as more dangerous than it is. To further discredit Todd's comments, Oliver uses a popular cultural allusion to remind his audience that a 2% mortality rate was "basically the entire plot of *The Leftovers*" before flashing an image of a despairing Justin Theroux. This HBO series, almost unrelenting in its darkness, showed characters unwilling and unable to move past the loss of their loved ones and accept the enigma of the departed. Oliver continues to put facts in perspective by reminding everyone that "a 2% mortality rate, if true, would be about 20 times higher than the seasonal flu" (3:05). What Oliver is doing here is a potent science communication strategy—using creative ways, such as analogies and visuals, to make numbers more comprehensible. His analogy is appropriate because a sizable portion of the American population struggles with numeracy, the ability to access, use, and interpret mathematical information. According to a report from the Program for the International Assessment of Adult Competencies (PIAAC), almost one in three U.S. adults (30 percent) has difficulty calculating whole numbers and percentages, estimating numbers or quantity, and interpreting simple statistics in text or tables. Or to put it another way, 62.7 million U.S. adults possess low numeracy skills. What this deficiency translates to, among other things, is an inability to conceptualize the significance of a 2% mortality rate. Oliver, then, is not only putting this mortality rate into perspective, but also targeting the media's irresponsible use of this heuristic to deflate the pandemic's seriousness. In a much later episode (7.10), Oliver uses a similar tactic to put a human face to the numbers. That is, rather than announcing that the coronavirus death total has just reached 65,400, he explains that in just three months, this disease has killed more Americans than those in the Vietnam War, an event cemented in the American cultural consciousness.

In critiquing the current administration's response to the coronavirus, Oliver keeps the focus on the response to the pandemic. That is, instead of making *ad-hominem* attacks against President Trump, Oliver invokes the public accountability frame for governmental leaders, using comparison and causal analysis to make his case. He first compares the current administration's fumbling COVID-19 response to those in other countries, such as Vietnam, which quickly rolled out an effective and catchy public health handwashing campaign. In contrast, Oliver positions President Trump as a leader who is not effectively using science in his decision-making, particularly by appointing Vice President Mike Pence, who has no medical training, as leader of the coronavirus task force. Oliver remarks that this decision is "more than just a lack of leadership, it is also concerning that Trump's main focus when discussing this virus seems to be downplaying any potentially bad news," such as his recent tweets that the coronavirus was under control, that it will recede in the warm weather, and that it was caused by the consumption of bat soup (14:00). A frustrated Oliver exclaims, that, for a public official, there is a grave difference between "lying about something that means nothing and lying about the spread of a deadly disease" (14:39). Oliver's point is that the president's irresponsible messaging and lack of leadership are creating an atmosphere where both the pandemic's seriousness and scientific authority are questioned. In doing so, the president is setting the stage for the acceptance of pseudoscientific explanations and the mainstreaming of dangerous alternative remedies (Jim Bakker's miraculous colloidal silver), which will exacerbate the current health crisis, if not create a new one. Oliver makes the case that both "trust in institutions" and medical authority, which are crucial to contending with the coronavirus, are being undermined by the Trump administration. At the end of the monologue, the host, acting as an explainer journalist, steps in to reenforce the authority of the CDC and his own version of public health messaging: "Don't be racist; Don't hoard masks; Check the CDC Website; Wash your hands regularly."

After this episode, unfortunately, the pandemic escalated. That is, by the filming of 7.5 (March 15, 2020): "COVID-19 Pandemic and the Prevention of COVID-19" (Coronavirus II), there were 3,000 new cases and 10 deaths in the United States, Europe was continuing to lock down cities and close borders, and airports were in chaos (Boschen). Oliver himself has been affected—confirmed cases in both his office and studio resulted in closing both locations. At the beginning, Oliver announces that his "staff has been working from home and we're currently taping this somewhere else with a very limited crew on this white void set . . . It kind of looks like the place movie characters go when they've just died." And, by the airing of the third segment of this series, episode 7.6 (March 29, 2020): "COVID-19 Pandemic Related Shortages and Social Distancing," there were at least 900 deaths in the United States (*The New York Times* and *Our World in Data*). The country was also at the beginning of a steep spike in cases, which would result in 2,289 deaths by April 17.

In 7.5, responding to the exigency of the situation, Oliver makes his message more urgent, his tone more somber, the pacing less frantic, and his content more focused. Even the comedian's crude homoerotic jokes involving actor Adam Driver fall flat, coming across as weak attempts at humor in an unbearable situation. Acting as an explainer journalist once again, Oliver summarizes the various coronavirus developments in the last few weeks, such as the cancelling of sports events and the stories of celebrities catching the virus, before offering his perspective: "We are clearly in the middle of a rapidly escalating outbreak" (3:24).

Relying on the public accountability frame, Oliver contrasts the pandemic crisis with the commander-in-chief's frequent inability (or reluctance) to communicate clearly: President Trump's mistaken claims that imports from Europe are being cut off, that insurers would waive copays for tests and treatment, and that Americans visiting Europe could not return home. Oliver is not just name calling here but framing the president's actions in terms of public accountability. Although President Trump, as the commander-in-chief, is responsible for messaging and action related to COVID-19, he repeatedly lies, denies knowing anything, and rejects responsibility. The president's irresponsible behavior, as well as that of other important public figures, is contrasted with effective examples of coronavirus messaging from both high and low: Fauci's honest testimony that the U.S. is failing at testing; and a video from a humble TikTok hamster. In the 12-second video that Oliver plays, a hamster advises people to wash their hands for at least 20 seconds, cough away from others, disinfect surfaces daily, wear a mask if you are sick, and stay at home. Oliver's satirical point is biting: this Tik-Tok hamster is a more responsible public health communicator than the president himself. Makers of homemade popular culture are doing a better job at covid communication than the White House administration and press office.

Understanding the communication crisis, Oliver implores his audience to be science communicators themselves. That is, to counter and compensate for both the president's lack of concern and "the harmful bullshit flying around," he invokes the personal and civic responsibility frame. He first humanizes the practice of social distancing, which is not just about protecting ourselves, but doing our civic responsibility to protect others. It is also about "slowing the spread of the virus so that it doesn't peak all at once and overwhelm the health care system" (14:40). Comparing spreading disease to disseminating disinformation, Oliver asks his audience to compensate for the president's lack of accountability. That is, if the president isn't going to be diligent when it comes to discounting lies and protecting the nation from the coronavirus, it is up to Americans to be responsible. Therefore, he asks for viewers' caution before "forwarding or retweeting stuff that you do not know to be true" (18:00). He also asks for their empathy and common sense: "You don't just get a flu shot for you; you get it for everyone else. We all have a real responsibility to one another right now because the choices we make in the coming days and weeks will contribute directly to how bad this crisis gets (18:30). His final message ties together personal and public responsibility: our small actions can, for better or for worse, affect the course of the pandemic.

The critique of president's contradictory messaging contradictory messaging continues in the next episode (7.6, March 29), such as his claims that the U.S. is fighting a war with this virus but there are plans to open up the country by Easter Sunday. However, here Oliver pivots to target both the president and conservative media's framing of the pandemic, which is acting as a red herring and impeding strategies to prevent the spread of the coronavirus. Framing the pandemic in terms of conflict (the health of the economy versus the health of the American population); and dire economic risk and catastrophe (quarantining will effectively close off the economy and cause escalating negative effects) is exacerbating the public health crisis. He targets those Republican pundits who question mask-wearing and store closures because they prioritize economic security over public health. For example, Oliver includes Tucker Carlson's interview with Lieutenant Governor Dan Patrick, who whines that no one reached out to him "and said, as a senior citizen, are you willing to take a chance on your survival in exchange for keeping the America that all America loves for your children" (7:01). This complaint is followed by a video of an angry Glenn Beck exclaiming, "I am not afraid to die; I am afraid that our nation might die" (8:28). Oliver reminds viewers that the attitude of Beck and others is selfish; they might think that by advocating to "open up America," they are preserving the future of their children and American life. However, they are actually volunteering American citizens to die. Oliver is effectively dissecting their propaganda here: messaging "designed to manipulate a target population by affecting its beliefs, attitudes, or preferences in order to obtain behavior compliant with [the] political goals of the propagandist" (Benkler et al. 29). By threatening that the economy will crash if people continue to isolate and businesses remain closed, these pundits are using fear to persuade people to drop preventative measures.

By analyzing the selfishness of these pundits, Oliver is again focusing on public accountability: many Republican political leaders and pundits, by pushing harmful propaganda, are rejecting their duty to fellow citizens. In contrast, Oliver implores viewers to ignore this "death cult" and follow protocols as strictly as possible to ease the burdens of healthcare workers and to protect human lives.

OLIVER AS INVESTIGATIVE JOURNALIST: ADDRESSING COVID-19'S SOCIOPOLITICAL ISSUES

Along with being an explainer journalist who communicates essential information about the coronavirus, Oliver acts as an investigative/watchdog journalist when he analyzes pandemic-related sociopolitical issues. In other episodes, Oliver draws attention to how the pandemic revealed weaknesses in the United States: a healthcare system that operates on efficiency and scarcity; states' rights that create a patchwork pandemic policy; and the country's obsession with the economy. In Coronavirus IV (7.8, April 12, 2020), VIII (7.16, June 21, 2020), and IX (7.17, June 28, 2020), Oliver addresses other systemic inequities and injustices in American society: the lack of respect for essential workers, the minimal unemployment safety net, the inhumane conditions in America's crowded prison system, and the lack of affordable housing and increased evictions. The pandemic, Oliver contends, has thrown a spotlight on the defects of various systems that are central to American life.

This section will analyze only one episode that addresses sociopolitical coronavirus issues, which is also a very emotional segment: Episode 7.16 (June 21, 2020): "COVID-19 Pandemic in Prisons and Jails." Here, Oliver shines a harsh light on how the inhumane conditions of American prisons have accelerated the spread of the virus. His highly organized monologue is divided into three sections: the mechanisms that allowed the coronavirus to spread so rapidly behind bars; the effects of the prison pandemic; and solutions for this crisis. This episode begins by following up a recent *New York Times* story about the alarming spike of cases in prisons: 68,000 infected inmates (a number that had doubled in the last month) and a 73% increase in coronavirus-related prison deaths. Oliver then announces that the five largest "clusters of the virus are in correctional institutions" (:46); and that there are 2.2 million people held in prisons, many of them in poor health (1:38), which makes this population especially vulnerable to infection. And in assuming the investigative science journalist role who recruits both the morality/ethics and public accountability frames, Oliver uses comparably dissimilar sources. He does cite legacy news stories, but he relies most heavily on *The Marshall Project*: an online, non-profit journalism organization that focuses on issues related to American criminal justice. This organization, which has won the Pulitzer Prize twice, has a goal to "create and sustain a sense of national urgency about the U.S. prison system."

Demonstrating this urgency himself, Oliver embeds several interviews revealing the conditions in prison (tiny cells), the unhelpful social distancing advice (telling prisoners to sleep head to foot in their bunks) (4:10), the rationing or lack of soap (story from the Brennan Center for Justice) (4:54), anguished (and angry) reports from prisoners themselves (5:28), and a *ProPublica* article on a prison having 2,000 coronavirus cases (5:55). Along with critiquing poor hygienic conditions, Oliver targets the lack of personal protective equipment (PPE), minimal tests, and improper quarantining locations (Those who test positive go not to a hospital ward but to isolation). His main goal, then, is exposing that the infrastructure of jails and prisons, which make them incapable of protecting people from disease, is worse than unethical: *it is a human rights disaster*. Despite our opinions of those residing in prisons and jails, we "don't punish people by giving them diseases" (2:18).

After highlighting these atrocities, Oliver provides sensible and moral solutions to this crisis: reduce the number and/or furlough prisoners, especially those who are near the end of their sentences or immune-compromised. He admits this solution is imperfect, but "the risks of carefully letting people out are vastly outweighed by the risks of leaving everyone inside" (13:32). Understanding resistance to this solution, he reaches out to those Americans who recruit the morality/ethics frame when justifying the existence of prisons. He understands that many hold the sentiment that "You shouldn't do the crime, if you can't do the time" (17:43). However, in "our current system, you're never being sentenced to time. You're being sentenced to a lifetime of social stigma, futile job interviews, and roadblocks to necessities like housing" (17:55). Because all this treatment is immoral enough, we shouldn't "be sentencing people to die from a virus. Because that's not justice, it's neglect" (18:03). In other words, the punishment of contracting COVID-19 while in prison is out of proportion to the original crime.

Further anticipating any objections to treating prisoners more humanely, Oliver blends matters of morality and public health. He stresses that the poor hygiene and crowded conditions of prisons are not only unethical, but also dangerous to the entire population. To make this claim, he targets the erroneous thinking that prisoners are outside the population, such as a California county's decision to exclude prison infection rates in its COVID count; and a revealing clip from the director of the Arkansas Department of Health (Nate Smith) who refers to prisons as high-infection settings that are fortunately "closed systems" (8:26). Oliver lets Smith hang himself on his own words, such as his assertion that it is not difficult to contain coronavirus outbreaks in prison "because people aren't going out and about. They're not leaving the prison" (8:18-8:43). Acting as investigative science journalist, Oliver corrects Smith's faulty messaging with facts. Prisons are not closed systems; people are definitely emerging from them (9:33). There are, in fact, 445,000 prison workers, who have reported 9,180 cases: "we might as well be handing them coronavirus gift bags as they leave work every day and head back out into the community" (9:54). Then the mechanism of disease is explained: unlike what Smith asserted, the virus *can* hop from prison to prison as inmates are transferred around, to rural hospitals that treat prisoners, and jails, which, in a typical week, book 200,000 people. Prisons are not only permeable, but also epicenters of outbreaks that infect surrounding communities—for instance, Cook County was the source of 15.7% of all Illinois COVID-19 cases.

In the conclusion, these two parts of the story—the immoral treatment of prisoners and the public health threat of prison outbreaks—are linked in Oliver's final claim that prisoners are STILL members of this society and that "We're all on this death cruise ship together" (18:22). The morality/ethics frame (prison conditions are especially inhumane in a coronavirus crisis) is united with the public accountability frame (we must act to amend these conditions and condemn officials who don't recognize that prison conditions can create a public health crisis). Also, in all three of these episodes on coronavirus-related sociopolitical issues (renters, prisoners, front-line workers), Oliver analyzes how the pandemic continues to reveal the inequities disproportionately faced by women, lower-income Americans, and people of color.

OLIVER AS WATCHDOG SCIENCE JOURNALIST: DEBUNKING CORONAVIRUS CONSPIRACIES

Throughout the entire COVID-19 series, Oliver regularly exposes and then corrects coronavirus-related information and disinformation, which was rampant during the pandemic. In February 2020, Christian Paz began compiling President Trump's biggest coronavirus mistruths. Almost immediately, there were false claims about the transmission and decline of the coronavirus, such as the announcement that the coronavirus would weaken in warmer weather (Feb. 7); assertions that the outbreak was only temporary (Feb. 27); claims that 99% of Covid cases were harmless (July 4); and statements that children were "virtually immune" to this disease (several times). The president also miscommunicated that coronavirus cases were decreasing (when they were actually increasing or spiking) (multiple times) and that hydroxychloroquine (a potent antimalarial) was a coronavirus cure.

Exacerbating the effects of the president's unscientific and irresponsible messaging were circulating global conspiracy theories. Probably the most ridiculous, yet dangerous nonetheless, were disseminated by QAnon, who used the pandemic as a wedge issue to promote their propaganda, such as further distrusting the "lamestream media," targeting minority communities, critiquing government overreach, and calling for extreme violence and civil war (ISD Global 1). Using the internet as its far-right megaphone, QAnon spread several coronavirus conspiracy theories: that it was an incurable bioweapon created by a secret government cabal to restrict personal freedoms and to institute martial law; it was manufactured and then dispersed by George Soros to destroy Republicans; and the virus was a ploy to destroy their hero, President Trump, and ruin his stellar economic record (ISD Global 9-10). Whereas President Trump had previously called climate change a "hoax," he did not overtly repeat these conspiracy theories. However, he made little effort to distance himself from this extremist group's messaging. In fact, LaFrance tabulated that President Trump, without confirming conspiracy theories, still retweeted 145 messages about them.

This polluted media environment correlated with intensifying political polarization about the severity of the virus as well as the strategies for mitigating it. A CBS News-YouGov poll found that 57% of Republicans surveyed believed that the death count (which at that time was 176,000) was acceptable whereas 43% said it was unacceptable. In contrast, 90% of polled Democrats stated that these deaths were not at all acceptable. Even more disparate were fears about contracting the coronavirus—with 89% of Democrats expressing mild to serious concern but only 49% of Republicans doing so. The majority of Republicans polled were also more likely to believe the conspiracy theory that the mainstream media was actually over-reporting the death toll. Many Republicans, as they had done before with climate change, began to perceive the pandemic crisis as exaggerated and the coronavirus rhetoric as alarmist. These same people began to paint scientists as politically biased, on the side of liberals.

Responding to the accelerating infodemic, Oliver assumes the watchdog science journalist role and targets disseminators of disinformation, misinformation, and conspiracy theories in episode 7.9 (April 19, 2020): "Misinformation related to the 2019–20 coronavirus pandemic; episode 7.10

(May 3, 2020): "COVID-19 testing" ("Coronavirus VI"); and episode 7.18: "Conspiracy Theories about COVID-19." Nisbet defines the watchdog role as one in which the journalist "holds scientists, scientific institutions, industry and policy-oriented organizations to scrutiny." This role can also involve critiquing "scientific institutions and the scientific community" as well as "individuals or groups making false claims, and over social actors intervening in science policy discussions." Oliver takes on all these tasks here.

Both episodes 7.9 and 7.10 target the purveyors of coronavirus dis and misinformation. In Episode 7.9, released about the same time as the first major COVID-19 spike (an average of about 2,000 deaths a day in the last week), Oliver announces the effects of circulating coronavirus myths: 40% of Americans now believe the coronavirus is "less deadly than or just as deadly as the flu." This attitude, Oliver advises, is self-defeating; it will extend the pandemic and keep us at home longer. Thus, this episode is dedicated to dissecting one of the main causes of disinformation: those various right-wing bubbles who are using the uncertainty frame and spreading coronavirus conspiracies. In the uncertainty frame, communicators describe science issues in terms of contradictory messaging or gaps in research. Certain Republican messengers, for instance, have regularly framed the climate change crisis in terms of uncertainty: the research is questionable, all the facts are not yet in, and there is no scientific consensus. As a result, they then argue, the reality of anthropogenic climate change remains a debate, so policies to address it are unnecessary. For Mooney, wielding the uncertainty frame amounts to political science abuse, which is "any attempt to inappropriately undermine, alter, or otherwise interfere with the scientific process, or scientific conclusions, for political or ideological reasons" (*War* 17). As the coronavirus pandemic raged on, certain commentators continued to question the severity of the disease, the accuracy of the science, the efficacy of vaccines, and the timeline of their administration. Framing the coronavirus in terms of uncertainty allowed interested parties to question the legitimacy of its science, opening the door to pseudo-scientific explanations, conspiracy theories, and alternative cures.

Appropriately, Oliver's biggest targets in this episode are pillars of the rightwing media ecosphere who are exaggerating uncertainty about the coronavirus. He first aims at Limbaugh, who, in labeling the coronavirus the 19th version of the common cold, folded the pandemic into his own personal narrative: the four corners of deceit (government, academia, science, and the media). Or to put is another way, there is a vast conspiracy in which these four groups are lying about the state of the coronavirus science to restrict American freedoms. Fox News' hypocritical use of the uncertainty frame is exposed: while instituting preventative measures at their own studios, network hosts continued to push the narrative that the science was unclear and that deaths were exaggerated. Even worse than the effects of these conspiracy theories on the American people, Oliver warns, are the effects on the president itself, who regularly receives his talking points from Fox News. Noting that the "feedback loop between Fox News and Trump has run way ahead of the science here" (13:44), Oliver points out that the network's various hosts dangerously promoted the alternative cure of hydroxychloroquine over 300 times. Invoking the president's lack of accountability once again, the host exclaims that what the nation has is "a network and a president who thrive on division feeding on one another at a time when we desperately need a unified response to a public health crisis" (17:58).

What Oliver is brilliantly explaining in this segment, in lay-person's terms, is Fox's role as the main player in a radicalized right-wing media ecosystem that "differs categorically from the rest of the media environment" (Benkler et al. 13). According to these authors, the right-wing media ecosystem is more susceptible to lies and mistruths because of a) the amplification effect of Fox News, which repeats and circulates questionable stories and conspiracies, or "fertilizes and distributes the lies" (Rabin-Havt 5) such as the "deep state"; and b) the lack of internal mechanisms that correct and retract faulty journalism. That is, in isolated right-wing media ecosystem, there is no motivation for its inhabitants to check partial truths or halt the dissemination of fake news. Because of this media ecosystem's low journalism standards, which contribute to its popularity, viewers are encouraged to believe ludicrous and bizarre conspiracies, such as Obama's death panels—but also dangerous ones, such as taking untested coronavirus treatments (from bleach to antimalarial drugs) as opposed to wearing masks or getting vaccinated. These conspiracies flourish because of the dynamic called "the propaganda feedback loop" (Benkler et al. 33) that names, confirms, and delivers identity-confirming news to audiences as well as the corresponding politicians, elites, and reporters who align with and then reaffirm these views. Furthermore, all the players in this loop rarely move outside it to seek alternative viewpoints. In this episode, and in 7.10 (May 3, 2020): "COVID-19 Testing," Oliver shows this propaganda feedback loop in action—in hope that his viewers will take on the role of science communicators themselves, exposing this loop to those trapped in and by it.

Oliver takes a slightly different approach in Episode 7.18 (July 19, 2020), dissecting conspiracy theories with the intent of turning his audience members into science communicators themselves. Beginning by citing *The Atlantic*'s claim that "COVID-19 has created a perfect storm for conspiracy theorists" (1:13), Oliver shows footage of the most prevalent coronavirus myths (the virus was created in a lab as biological warfare, invented by the pharmaceutical industry to create a market for vaccines, or invented to control the American people). Despite their ridiculousness, these theories are dangerous. For instance, after being released online and shared via social media platforms, the 26-minute documentary video *Plandemic* was viewed over 8 million times (2:35). *Plandemic,* an example of skilled social engineering (Nazar and Pieters), manipulated "low-reach social media users to mass share the documentary, effectively subverting efforts to gatekeep its information. Second, the campaign amplified negative sentiments regarding vaccination and containment measures among conspiracy theorists" (Nazar and Pieters). Some of *Plandemic*'s conspiracy theories were that the outbreak was planned, the virus was not deadly, mask-wearing activated our own virus, and beaches contain healing microbes. The rapid dissemination of this documentary impacted attitudes toward preventing the coronavirus and trusting health authorities. For instance, Oliver highlights how this film sparked the trending hashtag "filmyourhospital," which encouraged people to enter hospitals looking for infected patients. "Even if only a fraction of Americans succumbing to them ignore best practices, such as social distancing," Oliver explains, there will be consequences. However, rather than blast conspiracy-believers, he tries to build a bridge to them, even admitting his own weakness to one—that the royal family murdered Lady Di.

Assuming the roles of both explainer and watchdog science journalist, Oliver summarizes scientific research on the appeal, identification, and refutation of conspiracy theories. After citing a study that over half of Americans believe in at least one conspiracy theory, Oliver explains their mechanism. First, conspiracy theories not only help explain a chaotic world but also appeal to proportionality bias (4:47) —the tendency for people to believe that big effects must have big causes. For instance, a tragic phenomenon like a pandemic is easier to attribute to massive causes (a devious plan involving hundreds of global elites, for instance) than to the combination of an evolved, contagious virus and poor preventative health measures. Conspiracy theories are also attractive because they are self-sealing (10:33); any criticism of the theory becomes evidence that the conspiracy is even larger than imagined.

Oliver also addresses the historical basis of these theories and their connection to global health crises (the bubonic plague, the Spanish flu), referencing sources from *Vox*, *Forbes*, and the *History Channel*. Although pandemic-related conspiracy theories are not novel, what is new, thanks to the internet, is the rapidity of their spread and the breadth of their influence. Instead of satirizing these conspiracies, which is what Oliver would normally do, he requests that his viewers be patient when confronting them and their believers; that is, "[i]t's going to be incumbent on us as individuals to spot these theories and treat them with a skeptical eye before we believe them. Or, indeed, before we spread them around" (5:00). He provides viewers with three basic questions to debunk conspiracy theories: Is there a rational non-conspiracy explanation? Has this theory been held up to scrutiny by experts? How plausible is this conspiracy as a practical matter? To illustrate the first question, Oliver uses a striking visual—a map showing the seeming correlation between 5G maps and coronavirus outbreaks. Critical thinking, however, reveals that in these maps, the third underlying factor is population density. Rather than use the term "spurious correlation," Oliver simply shows how charts can lie. Personal and public accountability frames regularly merge in this monologue—in our individual communications, we are all responsible for recognizing and defusing conspiracy theories to prevent the worsening of the pandemic crisis.

Compared to other segments, Oliver's call to action here is lengthier and more involved, one that matches the gravity of the subject. He reminds his viewers that the popularity of *Plandemic* proved that social media companies can only intervene so much, so we must take it upon ourselves to communicate with conspiracy-theory believers so that coronavirus containment efforts are not derailed. Referencing science communication experts John Cook and Stephan Lewandosky, Oliver asserts that the most effective way to reach conspiracy theorists is not to shame or insult them, but to practice empathy, meet them where they are, and "nudge them to think more critically" (18:18). To demonstrate this strategy, he pieces together messages from approachable celebrities (Alex Trebek, John Cena, Paul Rudd, Catherine O'Hara, Billy Porter), who building bridges to conspiracy holders in different population groups. Together, they all gently and humorously provide advice on investigating sources before forwarding them to friends and family. Paul Rudd adds that you can recognize a truthful story if "a majority of trusted sources agree on it." "And finally," chimes in Billy Porter, "Think critically." Then, all the celebrities offer versions of this positive affirmation: "You're smart!" Indeed, Oliver has always motivated his viewers to act, but this segment marks one of the few times he provides them with resources (a reference to Lewandosky and Cook's *The Conspiracy Theory Handbook* and a link to the True True Truth, which contains longer versions of these celebrity videos) so that they can be empathetic, public science communicators themselves.

OLIVER'S SCIENCE JOURNALISM AS A RESOURCE
(REVISE BUT DON'T MAKE LONGER!)

In 2020, then, corrupted presidential messaging, misinformation, disinformation, and circulating conspiracy theories contributed to significant numbers of people resisting public health measures, such as refusing to wear masks, practice social distancing, and avoid large crowds. The actions (and inactions) of certain Americans would eventually lead to the rapid spread of the coronavirus in the Northeast along with several surges, predominantly in Republican-dominated regions (Jones). In the early days of this crisis, John Oliver dedicated several Season 7 episodes of *Last Week Tonight*, adopting what the writer sees as various science journalist roles. Throughout these episodes, Oliver communicates accurate information, incorporates reputable sources, appropriately frames facts, exposes mental shortcuts that are distorting coronavirus communication, and builds bridges to his viewers. Admittedly, this writer is ascribing these roles to Oliver, who has not admitted he is a journalist, let alone a science journalist. But he has openly confessed his fears about the pandemic, such as in an interview with Seth Meyers shortly after his third remote show (March 26). When asked about his panic level, on a scale of Trump losing the 2020 election to Trump winning four terms, Oliver said "3.5" (3:43). Rather than dwell on these fears, however, I believe Oliver put them to work in his science communication efforts.

Why do his efforts matter? Despite the fact that Oliver's HBO program attracts a left-leaning audience who might not need persuading about the pandemic, and despite the risk of regularly targeting the Trump administration, the comedian is not merely preaching to his limited choir. That is, Oliver is a public intellectual with significant reach. Whereas his HBO audience averages about 1.0 million views in real time, his

Last Week Tonight YouTube channel, which had 6.6 million subscribers in 2020, now has 9.03 million. These coronavirus videos, which had between 5 million and 15 million views, spread accurate information far past the eyes and ears of his original HBO subscribers. Being on YouTube, which Burgess and Green appropriately describe as "post-television" (25), Oliver amplifies his messages and extends his audience. On this channel reside many fans who can watch Oliver's program when it suits them and then actively share its content through social media, extending its influence, or reach. Although President Trump's supporters, conspiracy believers, and vaccination opponents might never intentionally watch *Last Week Tonight*, they might stumble across Oliver's videos on the internet or receive them from peers. Yes, they might be offended by the anti-Trump administration rhetoric, commenting angrily, but at least, in watching, they have momentarily left their echo chambers. Maybe, for even a few, these messages resonated, making a dent in that feedback loop.

Regardless, Oliver's coronavirus videos offer helpful mental heuristics for framing the pandemic in terms of personal responsibility and ethics; and they promote strategies that encourage thinking critically and debunking conspiracy theories. In our post-truth world, then, Oliver's coronavirus episodes remain invaluable resources for us to watch, to appreciate, to analyze, and to share.

WORKS CITED

Benkler, Yochai et al. *Network Propaganda: Manipulation, Disinformation, and Radicalization in American politics.* Oxford UP: 2018.

Bos, Mark, and Frank Nuijens. "Science Journalism." *Science*

Communication: An Introduction, edited by Frank Van Dam, Liesbeth de Bakker, Anne M Dijkstra, and Eric A Jensen, pp. 119-143.

Boschen, Austin. "Over 3,000 Cases in the U.S.; Airport Chaos Due to New Screenings." NBC News, 16 March 2020, https://www.nbcnews.com/health/health-news/live-blog/2020-03-15-coronavirus-news-n1159296. Accessed 24 July 2022.

Boykoff, Maxwell T., and Jules M. Boykoff. "Balance as Bias: Global Warming and the U.S. Prestige Press." *Global Environmental Change*, vol. 14, no. 2, 2004, pp. 125-136, *ProQuest*, https://doi.org/10.1016/j.gloenvcha.2003.10.001

Brewer, Paul R., and Jessica McKnight. "Climate as Comedy: The Effects of Satirical Television News on Climate Change Perceptions." *Science Communication*, vol. 37, no. 5, 2015, pp. 635-657, doi:10.1177/1075547015597911.

Burgess, Jean. E., and Joshua B. Green. *YouTube: Online Video and Participatory Culture.* Polity: 2010.

Ceccarelli, Leah. "Manufactured Scientific Controversy: Science, Rhetoric, and Public Debate." *Rhetoric and Public Affairs*, vol. 14, no. 2, 2011, pp. 195-228. doi:10.1353/rap.2010.0222

Coleman, Justine. "57 percent of Republicans say coronavirus death toll is acceptable." *The Hill*, 23 August 2020, https://thehill.com/policy/healthcare/513301-57-percent-of-republicans-say-coronavirus-deaths-have-been-acceptable

Death List 2022, The. www.deathlist.net. Accessed 28 August 2020.

Feldman, Lauren, and Dannagal G. Young. "Late-Night Comedy as a Gateway to Traditional News: An Analysis of Time Trends in News Attention Among Late-Night Comedy Viewers During the 2004 Presidential Primaries." *Political Communication*, vol. 25, no. 4, 2008, pp. 401-422.

Fung, Katherine. "John Oliver & Bill Nye School Climate Change Skeptics on 'Last Week Tonight.'" *Comedy | Huffpost*, 23 August 2020, https:www.huffingtonpost.com/2014/05/12/john-oliver-climate-change-debate_n_5308822.html

Galliah, Shelly Anne. *"YOU DON'T NEED PEOPLE'S OPINIONS ON A FACT!": SATIRICAL COMEDY CORRECTS CLIMATE CHANGE DISINFORMATION.* Open Access Dissertation, Michigan Technological University, 2020. https://doi.org/10.37099/mtu.dc.etdr/1022

Guthrie, Marisa. "John Oliver on the Luxurious 'Freedom' of HBO, His Complicated Relationship with NYC." *The Hollywood Reporter*, 16 May 2014. https://www.hollywoodreporter.com/news/john-oliver-luxurious-freedom-hbo-696165. Accessed 19 July 2019.

National Center for Education Statistics. "Adult Numeracy in the United States." Data Point. September 2020. https://nces.ed.gov/pubsearch/pubsinfo.asp?pubid=2022004. Accessed 24 Aug. 2022.

ISD Global. "Far-right mobilization." COVID-19 Disinformation Briefing No. 2." https://www.isdglobal.org/isd-publications/covid-19-disinformation-briefing-no-2/

Jones, Bradley. "The Changing Political Geography of COVID-19 Over the Last Two Years." *Pew Research Center*, 3 March 2022, https://www.pewresearch.org/politics/2022/03/03/the-changing-political-geography-of-covid-19-over-the-last-two-years/. Accessed 24 July 2022.

Kastrenakes, Jacob. "FCC Received a Total of 3.7 million Comments on Net Neutrality," *The Verge*, 16 Sept. 2014, https://www.theverge.com/2014/9/16/6257887/fcc-net-neutrality-3-7-million-comments-made. Accessed 2 January 2018.

LaFrance, Adrienne. (2020, June). "The Prophecies of Q." Shadowland | *The Atlantic*. https://www.theatlantic.com/magazine/archive/2020/06/qanon-nothing-can-stop-what-is-coming/610567/

Lakoff, George. *Don't Think of an Elephant! Know Your Values and Frame the Debate.* Chelsea Green Publishing, 2004.

Lewandosky, Stephan, and John Cook. *The Conspiracy Theory Handbook. George Mason University Center for Climate Change Communication*, 2020. https://www.climatechangecommunication.org/conspiracy-theory-handbook/.

Luckerson, Viktor. "How the 'John Oliver Effect' Is Having a Real-Life Impact." *Time*, 10 January 2015, https://time.com/3674807/john-oliver-net-neutrality-civil-forfeiture-miss-america/. Accessed 12 August 2020.

Marshall Project, The. https://www.themarshallproject.org/. Accessed 23 Aug. 2022.

McCormick, Craig. *The Science of Communicating Science:*

The Ultimate Guide. CSIRO Publishing, 2019.

Meyers, Seth. "John Oliver Shares How Panicked He Feels About Coronavirus." *Late Night with Seth Meyers. YouTube,* 27 March 2020, https://www.youtube.com/watch?v= DuzEd1EbT88

Mooney, Chris. "John Oliver and Bill Nye Show Why Cable News Climate "Debates" are So Ridiculous." *Grist,* 12 May 2014, https://grist.org/climate-energy/john-oliv er-and-bill-nye-show-why-cable-news-climate-debates-are-so-ridiculous/.

Mooney, Chris. *The Republican War on Science.* Basic, 2005.

Nazar, Shahin, and Tony Pieters. "Plandemic Revisited: A Product of Planned Disinformation Amplifying the COVID-19 'Infodemic.' 14 July 21, *Public Health,* https:// doi.org/10.3389/fpubh.2021.649930

New York Times and *Our World in Data.* "Coronavirus in the U.S.: Latest Map and Case Count." 28. Aug. 2022, The New York Times, https://www.nytimes.com/interactive /2021/us/covid-cases.html.

Nisbet, Matthew. "The Science Journalist Online: Shifting Roles and Emerging Practices." *WebNortheasternEdu,* 11 Oct. 2011, updated 2 May 2020, https://web.northeast-ern.edu/matthewnisbet/2011/10/01/the-science-jour-nalist-online-shifting-roles-and-emerging-practices/.

Nisbet, Matthew. "Communicating Climate Change: Why Frames Matter for Public Engagement." *Environment: Science and Policy for Sustainable Development,* vol. 51, no. 2, 2009, pp. 12-23. https://doi.org/10.3200/ENVT. 51.2.12-23

Nisbet, Matthew. "Framing Science: A New Paradigm in Public Engagement." *Communicating Science: New Agendas in Science Communication*, Taylor & Francis, 2009, pp. 40-67.

Nuticelli, Dana. "John Oliver's Viral Video: The Best Climate Debate You'll Ever See." *The Guardian*, 23 May 2014, https://www.theguardian.com/environment/climate-consensus-97-per-cent/2014/.

Oliver, John. "Coronavirus: Conspiracy Theories." *Last Week Tonight with John Oliver. YouTube*, 19 July 2020, https://www.youtube.com/watch?v=0b_eHBZLM6U&t=1012s

Oliver, John. "COVID-19 Pandemic and Governmental Response in the US." *Last Week Tonight with John Oliver. YouTube*, 1 March 2020, https://www.youtube.com/watch?v=c09m5f7Gnic&t=418s.

Oliver, John. "COVID-19 Pandemic and the Prevention of COVID-19." *Last Week Tonight with John Oliver. YouTube*, 15 March 2020, https://www.youtube.com/watch?v=_066dEkycr4&t=93s.

Oliver, John. "COVID-19 Pandemic in Prisons and Jails." *Last Week Tonight with John Oliver. YouTube*, 21 June 2020, https://www.youtube.com/watch?v=MuxnH0VAkAM&t=41s.

Oliver, John. "COVID-19 Pandemic Related Shortages and Social Distancing." *Last Week Tonight with John Oliver. YouTube*, 29 March 2020, https://www.youtube.com/watch?v=ElIf2DBrWzU.

Oliver, John. "COVID-19 Testing." *Last Week Tonight with John Oliver. YouTube*, 3 May 2020, https://www.youtube.

com/watch?v=7rl4c-jr7g0&t=26s.

Oliver, John. "COVID-19 Vaccine and Vaccine Hesitancy." *Last Week Tonight with John Oliver. YouTube,* 2 May 2021, https://www.youtube.com/watch?v=gPHgRp70H8o&t=84s

Oliver, John. "Effect of the COVID-19 Pandemic on Evictions" *Last Week Tonight with John Oliver. YouTube,* 28 June 2020, https://www.youtube.com/watch?v=R652nwUcJRA&t=208s

Oliver, John. "Essential Workers and Unemployment in the United States During the Coronavirus Recession." *Last Week Tonight with John Oliver. YouTube,* 12 April 2020, https://www.youtube.com/watch?v=6s4Bx7mzNkM&t=101s.

Oliver, John. "Impact of the COVID-19 Pandemic on Sports." *Last Week Tonight with John Oliver. YouTube,* 17 May 2020, https://www.youtube.com/watch?v=z4gBMw64aqk&t=39s.

Oliver, John. "Meat Packing During the COVID-19 Pandemic." *Last Week Tonight with John Oliver. YouTube,* 21 February 2021, https://www.youtube.com/watch?v=IhO1FcjDMV4.

Oliver, John. "Misinformation Related to the 2019–20 Coronavirus Pandemic." *Last Week Tonight with John Oliver. YouTube,* 19 April 2020, https://www.youtube.com/watch?v=dRFbwjwQ4VE&t=592s.

Oliver, John. "Mueller Report." *Last Week Tonight with John Oliver. YouTube,* 21 April 2019, https://www.youtube.com/watch?v=YMBj_tU7HRU&t=175s.

Oliver, John. "Net Neutrality I." *Last Week Tonight with John Oliver. YouTube*, 1 June 2014, https://www.youtube.com/watch?v=fpbOEoRrHyU&t=263s.

Oliver, John. "Paris Agreement." Last Week Tonight with John Oliver." *YouTube*, 4 June 2017, https://www.youtube.com/watch?v=5scez5dqtAc.

Oliver, John. "Statistically Representative Climate Change Debate." *Last Week Tonight with John Oliver. YouTube*, 11 May 2014. https://www.youtube.com/watch?v=cjuG-CJJUGsg.

Oliver, John. "Trump and the Coronavirus." *Last Week Tonight with John Oliver. YouTube*, 1 November 2020, https://www.youtube.com/watch?v=IuVo4fnpLC8.

Paz, Christian. "All the President's Lies About the Coronavirus." Politics | *The Atlantic*, 17 August 2020, theatlantic.com/politics/archive/2020/08/trumps-lies-about-coronavirus/608647/. Accessed 19 August 2020.

Peabody Awards. (2014). Retrieved from http://www.peabodyawards.com/results/null/1/2014/2014/title/asc

Poniezowik, James. "Unfortunately, John Oliver, You are a Journalist." *Entertainment | Time*, 17 Nov. 2014. http://time.com/3589285/unfortunately-john-oliver-you-are-a-journalist/.

Robin-Havt, Ari and Media Matters. *Lies, Incorporated: The World of Post-Truth Politics*. Anchor Books, 2016.

Suebsaeng, Asawin. "*Last Week Tonight* Does Real Journalism, No Matter What Oliver Says." *The Daily Beast*, 29 September 2014, https://www.thedailybeast.com/

last-week-tonight-does-real-journalism-no-matter-what-john-oliver-says

World Health Organization. "WHO Director-General's Opening Remarks at the Media Briefing on Covid-19." WHO, 11 March 2020, https://www.who.int/director-general/speeches/detail/who-director-general-s-open ing-remarks-at-the-media-briefing-on-covid-19-11-march-2020.

Zhang, Qifan. "Explaining the News Builds Audience for it." News Literacy 2016, 28 Feb 2016, http://projects.nyujo-urnalism.org/newsliteracy2016/topics/explainer-jour-nalism/

Table 1. John Oliver's Coronavirus Segments

Season, Episode, Date of Video	Name of Video	Total views right after release	Total views on July 20, 2022
Episode 7.3 March 1, 2020	"COVID-19 pandemic and governmental response in the US"	15 million	15,676,334 https://www.youtube.com/watch?v=c09m 5f7Gnic&t=418s
Episode 7.5, March 15, 2020	"COVID-19 pandemic and the prevention of COVID-19"	11 million	12,482,016 million https://www.youtube.com/watch?v=_066dEky cr4&t=93s
Episode 7.6, March 29, 2020	"COVID-19 pandemic related short-ages and social distancing ("Coronavirus III")	10 million	10,477,736 https://www.youtube.com/watch?v=ElIf2D BrWzU

Episode 7.8, April 12, 2020	"Essential workers and unemployment in the United States during the Coronavirus recession ("Coronavirus IV")	8.3 million	8,752,227 https://www.youtube.com/watch?v=6s4Bx7mzNkM&t=101s
Episode 7.9, April 19, 2020	"Misinformation related to the 2019–20 coronavirus pandemic ("Coronavirus V")	8.5 million	8,996,003 million https://www.youtube.com/watch?v=dRFbwjwQ4VE&t=592s
Episode 7.10, May 3, 2020	"COVID-19 testing" ("Coronavirus VI")	7.9 million	8,337,015 https://www.youtube.com/watch?v=7rl4cjr7g0&t=26s
Episode 7.12, May 17, 2020	"Impact of the COVID-19 pandemic on sports ("Coronavirus VII")	7 million	7,674,922 https://www.youtube.com/watch?v=z4gBMw64aqk&t=39s
Episode 7.16, June 21, 2020	"COVID-19 pandemic in prisons and jails" ("Coronavirus VIII")	4.9 million	5,408,190 https://www.youtube.com/watch?v=MuxnH0VAkAM&t=41s
Episode 7.17, June 28, 2020	"Effect of the COVID-19 pandemic on evictions" ("Coronavirus IX")	6.6 million	7,664,546 https://www.youtube.com/watch?v=R652nwUcJRA&t=208s
Episode 7.18, July 19, 2020	"Coronavirus: Conspiracy Theories" ("Coronavirus X")	6.7 million	12,007,315 https://www.youtube.com/watch?v=0b_eZLM6U&t=1012s

Nov. 1, 2020	"Trump and the Coronavirus" 7.28	8 million	9,048,339 https://www.youtube.com/watch?v=IuVo4fnpLC8
Feb. 14, 2021	"The Next Pandemic"	9.1 million	9,391,428 https://www.youtube.com/watch?v=_v-U3K1sw9U
Feb. 21, 2021	"Meat packing during the COVID-19 pandemic" 8.2		7,234,250 https://www.youtube.com/watch?v=IhO1FcjDMV4
May 2, 2021	"COVID-19 vaccine and vaccine hesitancy"		7,827,749 https://www.youtube.com/watch?v=gPHgRp70H8o&t=84s

"See Ya Real Soon": Destaging Fantasy in COVID-Era Disney World

By Vicky Pettersen Lantz

ABSTRACT

Disney Realism is generally effective at erasing present con-sciousness, but the specific nature and implications of Covid prevent WDW from discouraging guest awareness of it. The interjection of present real-world problems/solutions rup-tures fantasy. These barriers came in the form of distance, emptiness, and opacity. The social distancing guide markings on the ground, the shielding, the closed spaces, and the open backstage areas all created visible invisible barriers to the Disney park promise of the spectacular, the immersive, and the nostalgic.

Keywords: Walt Disney World, Covid, Tourism, Immersion, Fantasy, Theme park attractions, Theme park characters, Staged and themed spaces

"Nos vemos muy pronto": Destruyendo la fantasía en el Disney World de la era del Covid

RESUMEN

El realismo de Disney es generalmente efectivo para borrar la conciencia presente, pero la naturaleza específica y las im-plicaciones de Covid evitan que WDW desaliente a los hués-pedes a que se den cuenta. La interjección de problemas/ soluciones actuales del mundo real rompe la fantasía. Estas barreras llegaron en forma de distancia, vacío y opacidad. Las marcas de guía de distanciamiento social en el suelo, el blindaje, los espacios cerrados y las áreas abiertas detrás del escenario crearon barreras visibles e invisibles para la promesa del parque de Disney de lo espectacular, lo inmersivo y lo nostálgico.

Palabras Clave: Walt Disney World, Covid, Turismo, Inmersión, Fantasía, Atracciones de parques temáticos, Personajes de parques temáticos, Espacios escénicos y temáticos

"再见，欢迎再来！"：新冠疫情时代下迪斯尼世界的幻想破灭

摘要

迪士尼现实主义通常可以有效地消除当前意识，但新冠疫情的特定性质和影响却阻止了华特迪士尼世界（WDW）消除游客对新冠疫情的感知。当前的现实世界问题/解决方案打破了幻想。这些障碍的形式包括保持社交距离、场地空旷和模糊性。地面上的保持社交距离标记、屏障、空间关闭、以及开放的后台区域都为迪士尼乐园在壮观、身临其境和怀旧方面的承诺制造了可见的无形障碍。

关键词：华特迪士尼世界，新冠疫情，旅游业，沉浸感，幻想，主题公园景点，主题公园角色，营造的主题空间

*The appeal of Disney parks' version of senti-
mental utopia is so strong and the effect of the
utopian enclave so consuming that the parks
are perceived by patrons as spatially as well as
temporally removed from everyday reality. The
parks are true enclaves of the imaginary where
cares of the outside world are temporarily put
aside and forgotten.*

—Meyrav Koren-Kuik, "Desiring the Tangible: Disneyland, Fandom, and Spatial Immersion"

*I found that this time, understandably, there
was no escaping reality—even in "the most
magical place on Earth."*

—Tarah Chieffi, Insider.com, Opinion
piece, Mar 6, 2021

Disney parks center the tourist or guest experience
on lived fantasy. The theme parks stage lands, rides,
attractions, and atmosphere to embody and expand
Disney intellectual properties (IP). The theming and staging
enhance the idea of that what appears in the parks, and what
visitors can do/see, is fantasy come to life. Matthew Wilson
Smith frames the Imagineering term "Disney Realism" as the
parks "aiming to unify spectacle and spectator into a single,
idealized reality. ... this reality is located in a mythic time
that encourages nostalgia, hope, and fantasy while discouraging present consciousness" (Smith 268). Fans of Disney/
Marvel/Star Wars/Pixar can explore and indulge in IP-related stage shows, character meet ups, immersive play and rides,
and staged atmosphere. The theme parks even have their own

fan following, with recurrent visitors who Disney Bound[1] as a "Tower of Terror" bellhop or sing all the lyrics to "A Great, Big, Beautiful Tomorrow" on The Carousel of Progress. Disney parks, in the last few decades especially, cater to guests experiencing this Disney Realism—the spectacular, the immersive, and the nostalgic, sometimes all at once.

From late 2020 until late 2021 at Walt Disney World (WDW), all three often seemed literally and figuratively out of reach because COVID was/is part of collective present consciousness. The important reality of health measures ensuring public safety, like masking and social distancing, could not reconcile with the theatrical and fantastical realisms built into an immersive theme park. Disney Realism is generally effective at erasing present consciousness, but the specific nature and implications of COVID prevent WDW from discouraging guest awareness of it. The COVID protocols are necessary, and the parks still advocate on websites and in on-site signage/directives for tourists to follow safety measures. COVID required logistical changes to the park that could not be pushed into the background. Walt Disney World reopened after the initial COVID shutdown earlier than its global Disney-park counterparts and implemented several health and safety measures to redirect visitors, protect cast members,[2] and try to maintain some business during the first waves of COVID.[3] Most COVID protocols were relatively

---

1 Bounding is a fan phenomenon: "To Disney Bound is to go into the parks in twenty-first century attire that reflects the coloring, patterns, or general makeup of a Disney character. ... Bounders visit and interact in the Disney environment as tourists, not as the characters, but they do pay homage by using clothing to reflect their interest in or admiration for a character" (Lantz, 1343-44).

2 Disney refers to its employees as "cast members."

3 Many protocols and precautions were largely gone by December 2021. Visitors can still see some evidence of where line markers were or some

short-lived or ephemeral, with stage and fireworks shows running again and social distancing markers now merely discolorations on the ground. The parks, like mass collective imagination, want COVID reminders to be something past-tense or temporary or historical, or that never happened in the first place. Disney often maneuvers around complex socio-political and environmental concerns, or other nebulous problems by offering guests immersion into fantasy and away from present consciousness. COVID safety protocols directly influenced or interfered with immersive theming.

Part of the issue was COVID's newness and novelty. The COVID protocols were/are disruptive because the parks did not have time to sanitize and fold into the fabric of their fantasy worlds, so these elements appear on top of or oppositional to the aesthetic theming and theatricality throughout. The collective trauma or disruption of COVID is ongoing and complex, and cultural juggernauts like the Disney company crafted several solutions to continue producing content and making profits, all while giving fans new and nostalgic experiences. The ways in which WDW attempted to evoke Disney Realism in a pandemic offer insight into how much staging and performance feeds lived fantasy in the theme parks. Disney Imagineering defines park development as "utopian in nature," which "carefully program[s] out all the negative, unwanted elements and program[s] in all the positive elements" (qtd. in Wallace 255). This idealistic approach to theme park creation does not factor in real-life, global events disrupting every crafted, staged element in the parks.[4]

---

rides still have some shielding, but by and large, most shows are open, and barriers are down.

4   Considering a global event like 9/11, there were substantial changes in WDW security that were highly visible and disruptive at the time but that have become less salient to tourists because cultures are desensi-

Masks, social distancing, changes to character meets, or closing attractions happen inside the parks in very visible ways.

The parks offer guidelines for lived fantasy, in what Jennifer A. Kokai and Tom Robson call "thematic invitations" (Kokai and Robson 19). In their discussion of COVID-era Disney park-going, Kokai and Robson posit that without invitations, "the tourist is no longer being offered a relationship, a relationship with a costumed character it is their prized turn to meet, within the dramaturgy of the shows themselves, or with the narrated structured day of a theme park visit" (Kokai and Robson 19). In the attempts to offer smaller experiences in place of character interaction/stage shows/spectacular experiences, the WDW parks[5] created instead feelings of obfuscation, which rescind the invitations or block the narratives parks offer guests. Following Smith's framing of Disney Realism, the interjection of present real-world problems/solutions ruptures "mythic time" and dilutes "nostalgia, hope, and fantasy." These barriers came in the form of distance, emptiness, and opacity. The social distancing guide markings on the ground, the shielding, the closed spaces, and the open backstage areas all created visible invisible barriers to the Disney theme park promise of the spectacular, the immersive, and the nostalgic.

DISNEY REALNESS: THEMED SPACES AND LIVED NARRATIVES

COVID-era Disney destabilized the standard practice of staging through multi-sensory scenic elements and performance

---

tized to post-9/11 security measures. In comparison to events like 9/11, COVID is still unique. A security checkpoint and bag search is limited to just outside the park, and security within the park can be hidden in various ways.

5   Walt Disney World is the only park I visited in 2021, going twice (May and December), so I am only discussing the COVID experiences there.

with live actors/workers. In quickly implementing COVID measures, Disney destaged areas of the parks by eliminating performances and character experiences and disrupting visual narratives. Destaging interrupts any attempts at authenticity and realism in themed spaces. Scott A. Lukas, cultural anthropologist and theme park theorist, details the importance of sensory experiences and staged elements for visitors when he states, "In the theme park and the themed casino, a new form of consumer authenticity is created. ... As the patron picks up on sensory cues, [they are] taken with the performative dimensions of the theme and the sense that things seem real or authentic because *they are happening*" ("Theming as" 81). His emphasized point is that guests accept all experiences as authentic because themed spaces actually craft / stage realness, even if the realness is based in fiction. That is to say, WDW relies on mythic, fictitious, or fantastical source material in the parks to actualize or materialize story-worlds fans and guests can occupy. Immersive elements provide realness to these narratives. Disney, as a contemporary company in the business of historical and fictional fantasy, struggles with how to reimagine immediate problems in its themed spaces.

The swiftness of COVID was a hinderance to the way WDW crafts and maintains fantasy illusions and attempts to off-set cultural critique. Disney Imagineers actively engage with *some* global concerns or avoid *some* criticism through interactive and immersive attractions. To fold environmental concerns into their sea and animal parks, the Disney corporation fictionalizes historically colonialized parts of the world and scripts these spaces with a peaceful, conservationist message. Animal Kingdom's Kilimanjaro Safaris, for example, offers guests the premise that the Harambe Wildlife Reserve will guide them through an African savannah. Cast members and the line queue emphasize the concept of being in Harambe, a fictionalized African community, and what work that community does to preserve African wildlife.[6] Much of the park, including Harambe, informs guests about conservation practices Disney does and how people can actively participate in global preservation. Animal Kingdom offers Harambe as an immersive Africanized space and hires African-born cast members and artists to offer "authenticity" to the land. The aesthetics, architecture, food, and soundscapes create an atmosphere of what guests expect of contemporary Africa. What the park avoids is any real narrative understanding or engagement with damning colonial histories, destructive global economics, etc. in favor of theming. Essentially, as Lukas states, "the emphasis in theming is representation, or how something is said, not what is said" ("Theming as" 81). Disney visually presents unique elements like African décor crafted from rubber and bicycle parts but does not explain *why* those recycled materials would be used in a neocolonial developing nation.

A similar practice happens when the parks attempt to downplay racism through "representation" with a character like Princess Tiana. The filmmakers held to the problematic notion that Tiana's race was not as key to her character as her personality or drive was, or essentially colorblind characterization. As Sarah E. Turner explains, "Color-blind racism denies difference based on skin color by simply refusing to see color; therefore, Tiana is 'just a princess,' not a *black* princess" (Turner 84). As with Harambe, Disney avoids factual trauma with Tiana. The movie does not engage the idea of Tiana's friendly/rich/white friends, racial tension in the Jim Crow South, etc. and the main villain is a Black voodoo priest. The

---

6   The original end to the safari famously showed animatronic poached animals to highlight the importance of conservation, but the scenes were deemed too graphic and cut before opening.

framing of Tiana as one of many princesses meant Disney could avoid direct engagement with racial concerns when convenient, but also market her as the first Black princess, arguably profiting off a fictionalized Black female body. This concept is not only troubling and tired, but Tiana's Blackness is a fundamental part of her selfhood for many fans, and her popularity and race cannot be understated in terms of importance.[7] Tiana immersive meet and greets in the parks create both a space of empowerment and racism.[8] Tiana never actually gets to be just a princess even if originally created through what Turner calls a "lens of color-blind ideology" (Turner 91). The presence of Tiana and Harambe Village speak to how WDW erase everyday reality and craft fantasies where discussions of history, trauma, and global concerns do not fit the narratives.

COVID restrictions disrupted these narratives and the ability of the parks to immerse visitors into assumed "ideology-free" utopias, following Koren-Kuik (150).[9] WDW removed live performances and character meets, which help establish and maintain narrative immersion. Lukas provides context for theming and immersion in six distinct categories: "Architecture, Material Culture and Design, Narrative, Technology, Performance, Guest Role/drive" ("Introduction" 5). All theme elements blend or work together to stage authenticity and encourage guests to embody the reality of the themed

---

7   As a Black character Disney property, her narrative served as a means of half-addressing/half-avoiding Splash Mountain after George Floyd's murder with Disney announcing a ride overhaul to create Tiana's Bayou Adventure.

8   Cast members have reflected on guest encounters when playing Tiana in meet and greets.

9   Assumed of course because the cultural standard set up in the Disney parks tends towards a heteronormative middle-class privileging European colonial narrative.

space. While Harambe Village still had the visual markers of a conservation-centric Africa, lived fantasy elements such as streetmospheres and outside performances were missing.[10] The Tam Tam Drummers of Harambe, "impressive musicians in *authentic* dress," set the tone of the village by calling guests to dance and perform with them ("Tam Tam Drummers," emphasis mine). WDW tells guests via the website that the drummers are authentic before they arrive and therefore set up the idea that Hamabre is authentic because real African citizens perform there. This premise feeds the guest role— "forms of phenomenology, psychology, existential state, and identity"—as visitors enter an immersive, though imagined, Africa ("Introduction" 4). The Drummers' absence during early COVID meant that live human interactions which convey Disney narratives was missing, and part of Disney guest identity/state was disrupted.

In *Fan Sites: Film Tourism and Contemporary Fandom,* Abby S. Waysdorf discusses the relationship between physical space and spatial transmedia in terms of Universal Studios' Wizarding World of Harry Potter, which shares ideological DNA with Disney in immersive theming. She suggests that theme parks "are specific places in which fantasies, mythologies, and cultural icons can be enacted and played with" (Waysdorf 90). Embodiment and play are inherently performative aspects of fan culture and theme parks like WDW offer guests a set stage for these fan performances. Theme parks use Lukas's grouping of Architecture, Material Culture and Design, Narrative, Technology, Performance, Guest Role/drive to

---

10 Streetmospheres is a portmanteau of street and atmosphere that Disney uses to describe performances guests could walk by or happen upon. The term was directly used for Old Hollywood performers in Disney-MGM Studios, but the company now uses it across the parks for a variety of performances and interactions.

establish full sensory sites. Many areas of the parks blend visual, aural, tactile, and olfactory stagecraft to encourage narrative play that helps guests have real sensory responses and feel real emotional investment. Waysdorf considers themed spaces to craft story-worlds, and "the story-world becomes immersive because it is inhabitable—as detailed as the 'real world' and shared with others as a sort of imaginary habitus" (92). Realness, in this context, is habitable space and WDW offers fans a variety of lived/habitable IP-related areas to explore. COVID and safety implementations made WDW spaces feel distant, empty, and opaque. These barriers meant the parks felt less inhabitable, and therefore less real.

ABSENCE AND STAGECRAFT: ARIEL'S GROTTO

Deep in the back of Fantasyland, in WDW's Magic Kingdom, visitors can find the princess-mermaid Ariel. The park website advertises the Ariel Meet and Greet as a genuine interaction with a real-life fictional fantasy: "*Venture into a seaside grotto*, where you'll find Ariel among her treasures. She has gadgets and gizmos aplenty, and she's always happy to make new friends—especially *human* ones" ("Meet Ariel at her Grotto," emphasis mine). Of course, meeting Ariel is real, in that it is an in-person interaction in the parks. But what the website implies is that visitors accept their narrative of a real grotto, with a real mermaid who wants more friends— human ones. This is typical of how Disney sells and narrates experiences inside the parks, as fundamentally real and true: Visitors meet Ariel-as-mermaid[11] in her personal space; the website does not say a "meet a white female cast member who fits the costume and wig in a staging area that looks like the animated movie." The general conceit in the parks is that

11 Guests can meet land/walking Ariel at some events and locations. The Grotto is mermaid underwater Ariel.

theatricality and staging do not exist; the adult tourist/fan accepts these experiences as real, and both guests and cast members ignore the obvious signs of their theatrical, staged nature. The pre-COVID in-park character meets feed that invitation for immersive play as visitors can touch and talk with the characters.

In fact, characters cease to be "characters," as that implies their fictive nature, but instead become real, *nonfictive* beings. Rebecca Williams notes this transformation, stating, "the theme park worker behind the mask or in the costume becomes erased whilst the character they are playing is the object of fannish adoration and celebrity reverence" (Williams 25-26). Adult fans in particular default to nonfictive relationships with characters on Instagram, and Ariel is just one example of how themed space and social media blend to commemorate meeting a real Disney princess.[12] People extend the dramatic staging and narratives inherent to meet and greets in the themed space of the Grotto to their social media. Twin users and Orlando residents, Kaitlyn and Skylar Dickerson, posted ten Grotto meet up pictures on their shared account @thenottwintwins to celebrate Ariel's birthday and stated "Happy Birthday Ariel!!!! 🎉 enjoy a few throwback pictures of us with her over the years!" (Kaitlyn & Skylar Dickerson). The pictures show a wide range of years and group members, with the main uniting factor being Ariel in her Grotto. It is apparent the cast members playing Ariel changes, but that does not matter because Ariel the live/d character is consistent.

User @mistthemermaid, a New York mermaid performer highlights that she and Ariel have shared physicality and

---

12 All Instagram posts referenced use Instagram's locator feature and posts list "Ariel's Grotto in the New Fantasyland" as the location.

experiences: "Remember that time we met Ariel, Caylis?! She was just the best, especially when we talked about our scales shifting into legs when we went on land!" (Mist the Mermaid). The conceit here is that Mist the Mermaid and Ariel share both human and mermaid abilities. Improv from the cast member means shared experience and makes *Ariel* "just the best," but not the cast member for improvising, reinforcing Williams' assertion of erasure. The posters accept the premise that they met the mermaid Ariel in her home and the images reinforce that idea, showing guests hugging, goofing, and relating to finned Ariel. Both posts also bring Ariel into their real lives. The Dickersons celebrate Ariel's birthday and show how often they interact. Mist, a professional mermaid performer, insists that she and Ariel share that trait, or at least both have fins. Ariel is both someone to meet in the parks and someone to fold into their lives outside the parks. The nature of mythic time and Disney Realism allow for this slippage. What happens to a princess-mermaid in a cave-like grotto during COVID? Like all character meets, she disappeared, awkwardly and overtly as the real-world crisis took over areas of the parks.

During 2021, the four WDW parks reallocated space, shut down experiences, and limited movement for safety, and in doing so, disrupted much of the cultivated Disney park narratives for visitors. In May 2021, there was no Grotto. As a means of social distancing, the Little Mermaid ride used Ariel's Grotto for a COVID back exit in order to spread out and separate guests (FIG. 1). This extended exit for guests covered the meet-and-greet area with pinned up cloth tarps. Not very fancy ones at that. This is unusual because Disney parks typically craft and stage work projects in a way to obscure park updates and maintenance and give guests something dynamic or themed in workspaces. These tarps are not that.

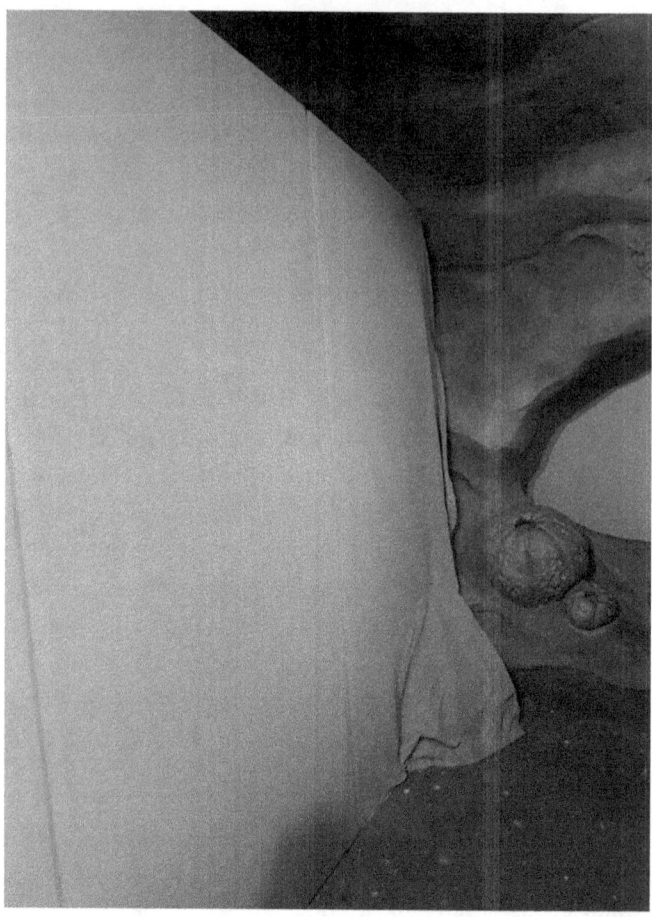

FIG. 1: The Character Meet and Greet stage, Ariel's Grotto, covered to make a back exit for the ride Under the Sea - Journey of the Little Mermaid, May 2021 (photo by author)

They are obvious, and very obviously covering up a previously used space. They indicate to guests that they are missing something. The tarps are a visible barrier to all guests, implying that this is an unused or unusable space. Any empty space could conceivably be said to be "unused." The problem with the Grotto is worse than that. The space was originally specifically crafted as a show space, a theatrical staging for Ariel visits. Its architecture was literally designed to focus audience attention at its staging area. With nothing in that area, the Imagineering is working against itself. The covering draws guest attention to the very thing the parks do not want people to look at, because looking at that absence only causes guests to ask why it is empty, allowing the present consciousness of COVID to intrude and rupture the fantasy.

The absence in the Grotto is less apparent for first-time or non-frequent visitors. Park fans know that Ariel is absent, as the Instagram posts make clear. Hints of her presence exist everywhere in this space, in the soundscape of Ariel's seabirds and waves and in the stage design of the shell lights and the sand/shell concrete flooring. For park goers in the know, Ariel is felt but invisible. It is fundamentally a "Little Mermaid" space, but without the titular character to make new human friends, it is just a hallway with some pinned up cloths. Even the immersive elements of hallway stage craft are disrupted by the tarps. The parks needed the additional exit space, and protected guests and cast members by eliminating the character meet, but the result of a hasty fix is guests seeing multiple indications of missing experiences. For recurring and first-time park goers, these spaces created a sensation of "not like you remember" or "something is off" throughout the WDW parks.

BACKSTAGE VISIBILITY: RISE OF THE RESISTANCE

In May 2021, small and large disruptions appeared everywhere in the parks, from the empty stages and the Voices of America singing outside to a total lack of international cast members in the World Showcase at EPCOT and WDW's most narratively immersive and fantastical ride having the entire plot interrupted. Star Wars: Rise of the Resistance plays into embodied fan/guest experiences in the story-world of the Star Wars franchise. Staging and theatrical elements make the queue line feel like an enclosed rebel base and before the physical ride starts, multiple performances immerse visitors into the story. Holograms and videos of Rey and Finn give specific duties to guests, along with a non-film character named Beck who informs passengers on his shuttle that they are rebel forces right before the shuttle is captured. Following that, First Order forces detain guests on an imperial ship that looks as impressive as scenes from Star Wars films. Rebels help guests escape to vehicles and that, technically, starts the ride. The pre-ride parts of the attraction return to Lukas's key elements of themed immersion: "Architecture, Material Culture and Design, Narrative, Technology, Performance, Guest Role/drive" ("Introduction" 5). The cast members, movie narratives, and ride mechanics working together to give visitors stakes, objectives, goals, and identity, all markings of performative authenticity, leading to a climax of intense immersion and spectacle of being held captive on a star destroyer. The verisimilitude of the ride defines the guest experience through markers of reality such as living human performers improvising with guests and highly themed stage spaces of the shuttle and star destroyer bay.

In her discussions of the Wizarding World at Universal parks, Waysdorf assesses the importance of these converging elements, or staging. She states, "The visitor knows that they are not actually in Diagon Alley or Hogsmeade, but there is no more 'real' version, and it is a physical experience with all the cultural markers of reality. This makes it a convincing pretense, one that matches the existing imagination with physical sensation" (Waysdorf 100-101). Guests, especially fans of Star Wars, accept on one level that the ride is fiction, but they indulge the performances and immersion because the attraction is marked with realism. Guests pair imagination with physical interaction to fully invest in the story-world. Adjustments made for COVID bypassed many of these elements, including the key plot point of the shuttle ride and capture, and disrupted this immersion. The line of guests did not become rebel fighters totally surrounded by the meticulously sculpted and designed Galaxy's Edge in Hollywood Studios, but instead were just tourists entering the literal backstage, an employee hallway that looked like an office building, before entering the star destroyer. Similar edits to immersive narratives happened in rides throughout WDW.[13]

The backstage area of Rise of the Resistance was jarring and broke with the aims of the ride, the immersion of a shuttle capture. The guest experience, or frontstage, works to highlight the alienness, the adventure, and the energy of being a rebel in Star Wars. The ride itself is situated in Galaxy's Edge/ Black Spire Outpost/Batuu, an area of the parks that is one of the most seamlessly immersive part of WDW. There is a sense of intentional staged authenticity in the ride, or following Waysdorf, no more real version of Star Wars exists outside this themed space. Tourism scholars have for decades relied on theatrical framing to discuss tourist spaces, with Erving Goffman, Dean MacCannell, and John Urry all framing the tourist quest for authentic experiences through frontstage and backstage spaces. David Weaver states that frontstage is, in terms of tourist sociology, "manipulated and

---

13 The Haunted Mansion includes a scene when guests cram into a stretching room where they first hear the voice of the Ghost Host. The new Run-Away Railroad usually has a scene with a movie playing before Goofy crashes through a wall. In May 2021, guests just walked through a big hole without explanation. The stretching room provides guests with a moment of terror and darkness before the ride starts and the missing scene in Run-Away Railroad sets up the narrative premise of the entire ride.

managed to accommodate tourists," and the backstage is the everyday reality. But these spaces are not always entirely separate (Weaver 154). Weaver explains that for MacCannell, in many tourist locations, "frontstages [are] decorated with artifacts from the backstage" to ascribe a kind of authenticity for the tourists, so they feel like they are getting some kind of true experience (Weaver 154). True experiences in Disney center on fantasy and hyper-reality.

Sue Beeton suggests theme parks also work towards staged authenticity, and in fact "issues of authenticity and reality become blurred and at times inverted in the theme park" (Beeton 187). Disney, like many locations, even sells the backstage. Guests can pay for special tours to see some of the "magic and secrets" in the parks. But access to those spaces is mediated and controlled. Those tours do not include an employee hallway or a plainly wrapped mermaid grotto that disrupt highly prescribed fantasy narratives. The context of encountering the backstage on a special tour is different. Guests pay extra money to seek out the backstage. In a ride like Rise of the Resistance, guests work hard to maintain their immersion.[14] COVID divergent paths present a backstage counter narrative, where guests who usually indulge in the Disney illusion have to confront a lack of Imagineering in the tarp-covered Grotto or a windowless cast member hallway. For the sake of expediency, the hope of temporariness, and the safety of people in the park, the key element of the Disney park experience, the lived fantasy and narrative invitations to embody fandom, were shelved. The parks, quick-

---

14 Even in the meticulously immersive Black Spire Outpost, guests would have to try *really* hard to ignore the thousands of other tourists around. In fact, in some ways, the more convincingly immersive these spaces become, the more dissonant the tourist's presence in them becomes. The number-one enemy of tourist immersion is the tourist.

ly, reframed highly personal immersive interactions. If some event or attraction was not totally shut down, then it was roped off and set away from guests. These distanced experiences, some highly controlled and some totally unscripted, hinted at promised fantasy without giving guests the opportunity to live in it.

DISTANCE: CHARACTER SIGHTINGS

Walking into Magic Kingdom in May 2021, guests saw mascot members of The Sensational Six[15] and cast members welcoming guests at Magic Kingdom, but they were set above and away from guests in the roped-off second story of the Train Station, with masked cast members below blocking guest access to stairs, creating an additional barrier. Guests saw, heard, and waved to them all, but were unable to get close for pictures or hugs or any level of one-on-one acknowledgement and interaction. The parks included some atmosphere/streetmosphere that recurring guests would recognize but that had been restructured for distant and mobile performances. The barbershop quartet, the Dapper Dans, rode a streetcar while singing. Characters appeared on balconies or in walking groups, but all were moving, surrounded/protected by masked cast members, and kept socially distanced from each other and guests. For Waysdorf, themed spaces need interactivity: "Other people create the sense that the Wizarding World is a lively and living space … To complete the sense of immersion, the space must be occupied" (Waysdorf 103). Occupation and collaboration are key elements to embodied fantasy in the parks, and that was unachievable as

---

15 The Sensational Six are core characters from classic Disney animation: Mickey Mouse, Minnie Mouse, Donald Duck, Daisy Duck, Goofy, and Pluto. Prior to Daisy's inclusion, they were referred to as The Fabulous Five.

guests could not physically interact with characters and characters could not interact with each other.

Character meet and greets are a big part of immersive guest narratives. The cast members create for visitors a brief moment of interactive, improvised fantasy. COVID protocols precluded all such meeting and greeting. Instead, the parks implemented character sightings of various kinds, some of which were in a way accidental. The parks deliberately created character sightings, but there was no schedule or planned structure for guests.[16] With meet and greets, visitors plan their trip around waiting and meeting specific characters they are fans of. It is a deliberate part of the park visit for many guests. In the COVID character sightings, characters just appeared at a distance in any available locations conducive to distancing, and if guests noticed, they might wave or take pictures, meaning "the character visit, a usually highly scripted private highlight of Disney park trips, was reduced to a rushed, impersonal photograph obtained by those passing by" (Kokai and Robson 17). The characters themselves benefit from the meet and greet locations, allowing cast members to evoke the world of the films or shows and offer guests glimpses into characters' private lives. As Kokai and Robson explain, "Characters were removed from any contextual theming or presentation, ripped out of carefully constructed environments that typically help construct interpretation" (Kokai and Robson 17). The insertion of characters into non-contextual spaces meant guests were unclear on how or unmotivated to interact with characters in their story-world or other imaginative ways.

In terms of verisimilitude, sightings are more "realistic" than a meet-and-greet, which has many elements that feel staged

---

16 As COVID protocols continued, some character sightings did get schedules posted to the Disney World website.

and structured. Darth Vader marching somewhere with his storm troopers seems more realistic than Darth Vader hanging out to snap some pics with guests. The character sightings share a lot in common with the illusory "naturalism" of viewing animals in a zoo. However, following Lukas, the performativity of character meets creates authentic guest experiences. He states, "Actors, workers, and performers in these venues use a variety of tools—costume, rhetoric and acting, and behavior—to better immerse guests" ("Introduction" 4). Seeing characters at a distances confines performance to only costume and behavior, eliminating rhetoric and acting. Distance offers naturalism, but not authenticity.

In Kokai and Robson's framing of character sightings, duration and distance are significant factors. They highlight a rushed and passing experience of selfies with guests in the foreground and characters in the background. EPCOT character sightings included a princess carriage, drawn by a large Clydesdale, carrying most of the princesses of World Showcase. In May 2021, guests could spot Belle, Aurora, Jasmine, and Mulan together. They appeared, with no announced schedule or timetable to help guests catch the moment; encountering a princess carriage was a happenstance rather than a scheduled event. The carriage was slow enough for pictures but no stopping and no talking. The masked cast members created visible-invisible barriers, as they often did, and formed a path, moved guests, and established a socially distanced bubble for the carriage. For a princess, riding in a horse-drawn carriage is a more extreme and compelling version of theatrical staging, in part because of the realness of the horse itself—live animals impart an immediacy to the realism of the staging. However, the lived fantasy and immersion are missing because of the lack of interaction. The princesses are too distant and moving too quickly to create a

sustained moment of participatory fandom. Instead of deliberately seeking out princesses to meet, guests had to be lucky
enough to not be in a line for a ride and be in that part of
World Showcase at the right time.

All the princesses together on the carriage further muddles
the story-worlds the parks work to create. In her discussions
of food and fandom, Williams suggests that sense of place is
key to fan engagement, and a sense of place is partly missing in the carriage ride. Meet and greets are themed spaces,
which, like themed food experiences, further "fans' immersion in a world" in part through "access, authenticity, and
the auratic" (Williams 26). Now the Disney Princesses often share space in consumer goods, such as toy sets, and in
the parks, in a show like Fantasmic! The princesses appear
together in specific all-park events, including special dining, parades, and stage shows. All-park events remind guests
of the Big Fantasy, a communal Disney identity. Meet and
greets do not overtly promote that communalism but focus
more on immersion and participation. In EPCOT, and films,
Mulan and Belle do not exist in the same place and time, but
rather have homes in their corresponding parts of the World
Showcase. The distinctiveness of the spaces and individual
guest access create embodied fan experiences.

What makes the princess carriage sighting feel even more
out of place or different is the COVID markers. As for the
princesses, they were obscured and distant versions of themselves. They waved, each from their own vinyl protected carriage row. Guest awareness of COVID leaks into all encounters in the park. Seeing something different like the princess
carriage with vinyl sheeting, guests cannot help but attribute
it to COVID. Pre-2020, seeing princesses riding around in a
carriage would not necessarily feel out of place or so prob-

lematic. WDW can institute safety protocols to mitigate the spread of the virus in the parks, but it's a lot harder to filter out guest awareness of the virus. The sighting lacked interactive qualities of a meet and greet, which occurs in a themed/staged space that reflects the character. It lacks the personal interaction and the indulgence of fantastic-reality.

On a more random and surreal level of distance, the character Joy (Fig. 3) from Pixar's *Inside Out* was just running around a fenced off field near "Journey into the Imagination." She was doing her own imagined play. She pretended to paint with a stick, she did ballet, she laughed to herself. It was a bizarre solo performance piece that included genuine expressions of fun and play. Unlike the princesses, who were contained within a moving stage, Joy was just let loose in a fenced area. Also, unlike the princesses, she did not wave or acknowledge guests. The character sighting here was as if guests were peeping into her personal backyard or imagination.[17] As Figure 3 demonstrates, few of the people nearby noticed Joy, which indicates the specific kinds of theatrical realism that WDW guests are accustomed to engaging with. While guests want something immersive and theatrically real, they also, paradoxically, want something bounded and structured. It is not a princess in a carriage coming through at random intervals that is less real, but rather it is the wrong kind of real or the wrong kind of theatre. Most Disney park fans only seek novelty and open-endedness in very specific ways structured by Imagineering and Disney institutional memory. Mostly what they want is structure and familiarity.

---

17 Joy was not the only character to have free rein of this area. Winnie the Pooh also ran around this space with a butterfly net. Whereas Joy was an abstraction of her character, Winnie was an infantilization, with very toddler-like energy and playfulness as part of the butterfly catching.

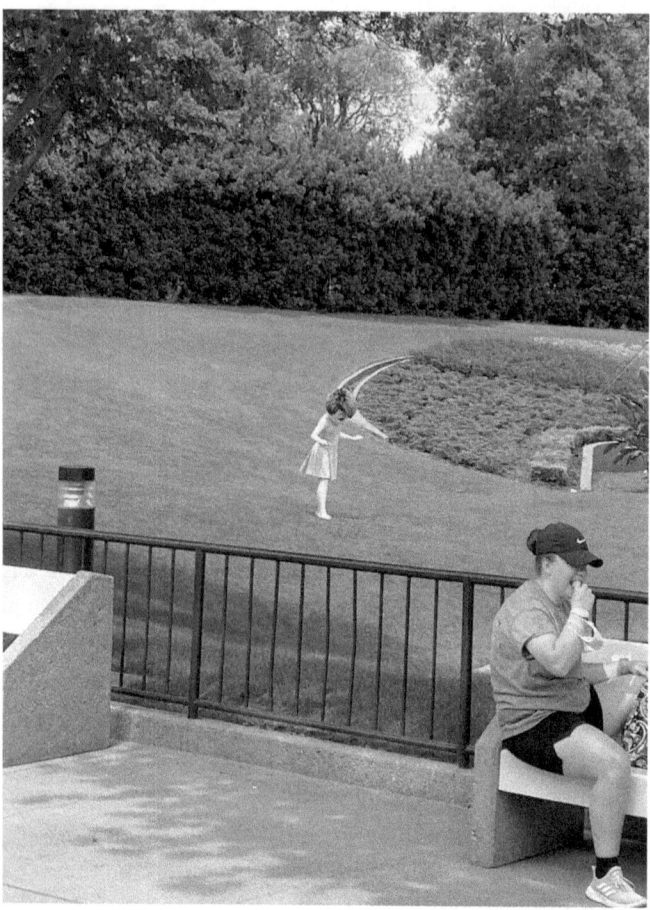

FIG. 2: Joy at play, with unknown guest not noticing the character sighting, May 2021 (photo by author)

Finding Joy in the field, moving through her own space and time was an interesting experiment in character sightings. Joy did not really act like her character in the film. That version of Joy is mission-orientated, memory-centric, and emotionally complex. Park Character Joy is a mascot character, meaning no moveable face and mouth, so she does not speak, so in all character meets, guests lost a sense of her film identity.

In this field, she was even more abstract. Character Sighting Joy was totally focused on imaginative play, without any attention or engagement with the reality of guests and theming around her. There was certainly a level of intimacy with the idea that guests were all voyeurs watching this imagined cartoon representation of the concept Joy doing ballet in the grass. However, in terms of the Disney theme park aims, Joy was very far away and not really engaged with guests. She was on some level immersive, but the short fence created a clear visible barrier, and along with the invisible barrier created by her absorption in her imaginary play, she became a kind of abstraction, something many guests did not register at all. Like everything in the COVID WDW parks, Joy was out of reach, non-interactive, and a less personal version of what she used to be at the meet and greets.

OPACITY: THEMED LINES

Seeing characters on street cars or carriages at a distance is not actually a new event in the parks; it was just rare to see as the *only* character experience. The least unusual element of the character sightings for many guests, fifteen months into COVID, was the clear plastic sheets between princesses. Clear plastic barriers, with all the implications of "look, but don't touch" was routine by May 2021 for people in daily activities like going into a bank, doctor's office, or grocery store. Clear plastic barriers offer up the idea of visibility and access, but the reality is a more obscured and blurrier version of an experience or interaction. As accessible to all park goers as WDW tries to be, the parks rely heavily on visual narratives to heighten the theatricality or immersion. Queues and pre-ride spaces reinforce narrative realness and give guests room to invest in the story-worlds. Being materially surrounded by theming creates "embodied, multi-sensuous and technologized performances through which people are actively involved in the world, imaginatively and physically" (qtd. in Williams 13). COVID visuals override active world embodiment on the part of guests. Inside buildings, each ride line also had clear plastic up, and depending on the ride vehicle, clear plastic attached to boats and cars to protect riders from each other's germs. The visible-invisible barrier of opacity is especially noticeable in the line and ride experience, or what scholar Tom Robson quipped on a Magic Kingdom visit as the cattle-chute experience when talking about Big Thunder Mountain's plexiglass line. The plastic tries to perform an impossibly contradictory function of being visible enough that guests feel comforted/safe but also invisible because WDW does not want guests thinking about COVID while in the parks.

Outdoor lines offered a very abstract but obvious barrier in the social distance markings on the ground (see Figure 3). These complicated pathways marked routes in which the parks limited guest physicality and interaction within the staged environments. The pathways themselves where not always clear, which is decidedly un-Disney. The Disney parks incorporate crowd management into the aesthetic design and immersive theming, and Imagineers study guest patterns to best control traffic flow, guest movement, and park narratives. Quick COVID changes such as these extended ad hoc pathway stickers did not encourage clarity or control. At the WDW parks in May 2021, about half of guests were still standing on the designated spots and half were meandering around the directional pathways. A lot of arrows and signage stating "please wait here" attempted to physically define the space, the lines, and the guests. To accommodate social distancing, the lines became much longer and occupied space that the parks typically use for thematic or dynamic environmental experiences. Immersive worlds like Toy Story Land and Galaxy's Edge had the entire *mise en scène* disrupted, or at least distorted, by the ground markings.

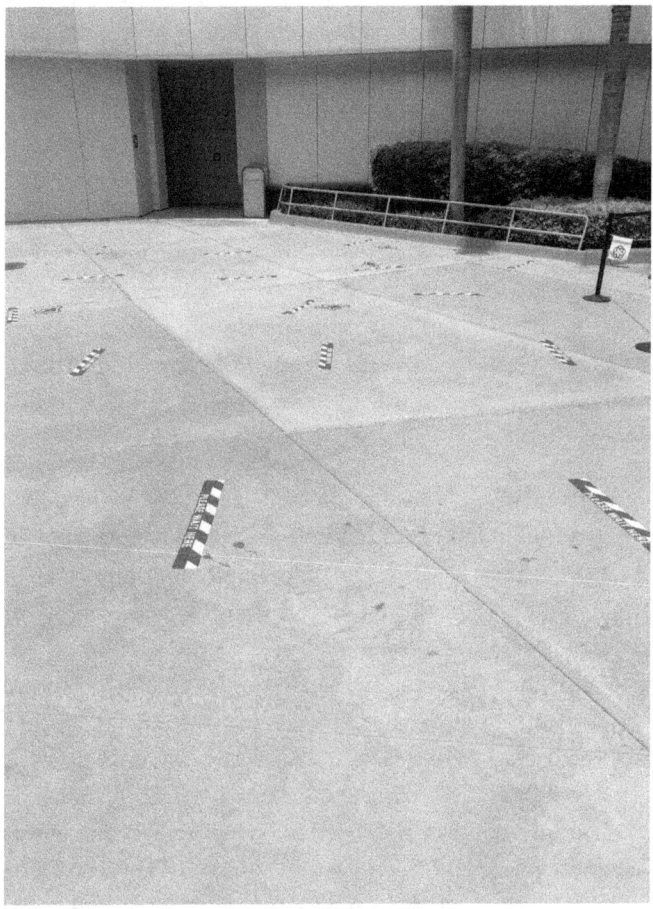

FIG. 3: The extended COVID line path outside Spaceship Earth, May 2021 (photo by author)

The line stickers in Figure 3 appeared throughout all the parks, regardless of theming. These markings, reminiscent of those in everyday spaces such as government buildings, classrooms, and restaurants, create unavoidable physical reminders of the pandemic and pull the usually fantastical space of WDW into the unpleasant concerns of the world outside the parks. Guests, at that moment in COVID, were just recently accustomed to wearing masks and standing away from people.[18] A new factor, which many guests had less experience with despite COVID-adjusted lifestyles, was the use of barriers in small, indoor spaces. Indoor lines in WDW typically use a tightly folded switchback formation to save space and to conceal the actual length of the line, but this format means guests repeatedly pass each other in very close proximity. For safety purposes, the clear plastic liners extended the height of the switchback railing, turning previously open-aired lines into closed spaces. This effect created the sensation of physically penning guests in within indoor lines and further disrupted the themed space and narrative.

By lacking visual clarity, the plastic barriers created the opposite-than-intended effect. Cleanliness, or the appearance of it, is historically a Walt Disney principle, and important to the WDW aesthetic pre-COVID. During the pandemic, plastic, face-level surfaces focus inadvertently more on germs and contamination. The plastic barriers were trying to achieve two mutually exclusive goals *vis-à-vis* their (in)visibility: they need to be visible in the sense that Disney wants concerned park goers to know that the company is taking responsible precautions, but they also need to be invisible so that guests are not reminded of why they need to take precautions. These barriers are contradictory in both function *and* purpose. The character sightings at a distance might be ignorable or more forgettable, but they are unambiguously visible, and theme parks are a highly visual medium. Additionally, all the charac-

---

18 These practices have greatly diminished, to the point that masking was rare in the parks by summer 2022 despite rising COVID cases.

ter sightings were outside, away from ride and attraction lines, so they were open-aired happenings. Within show/ride buildings, staging becomes central to themed narrative and entertainment distraction, so any disruption to the staging means guest experiences shift away from what Williams calls "bodily sensations associated with immersion" (Williams 12).

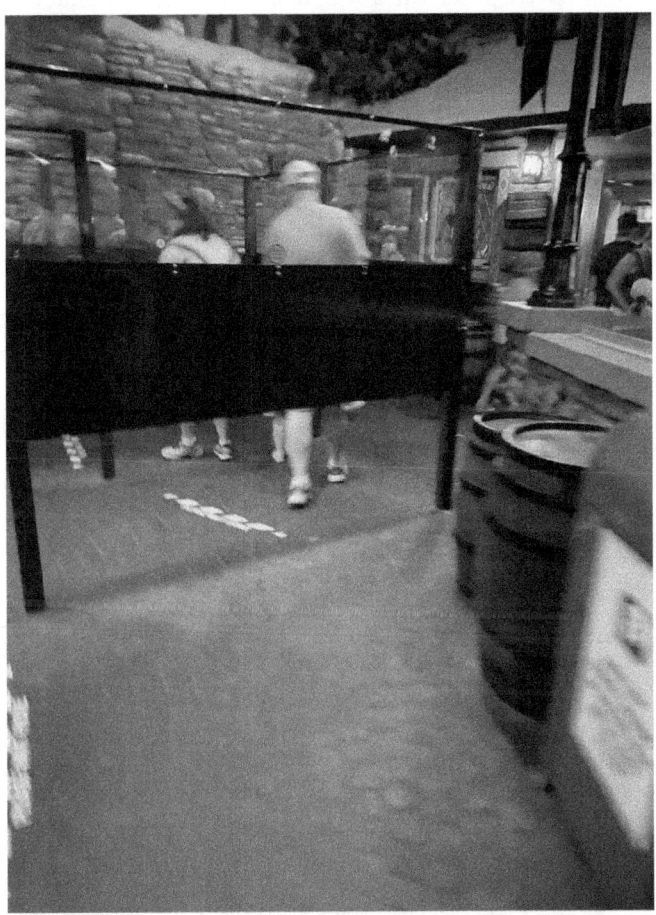

FIG. 4: The plexiglass switchback for the Frozen Ever After ride, May 2021 (photo by author)

Figure 4, the Frozen Ever After switchback queue, clarifies just how out of place the plastic barriers were/are,[19] and the reflecting lights and layers of glass obscure the highly defined environment. The staging of the space is reflective of Arendelle, the kingdom in *Frozen*, and includes simulation of natural stone and wood Scandinavian architecture. The old queue dividers were posts with a sculpted, somewhat old-fashioned look, connected by lengths of chain. These features were made of material objects that could conceivably exist within the culture and period the theming evokes. The new barriers created dissonance with that aesthetic. EPCOT put in new barriers which are clearly industrially made and lack the softer, organic shapes of the staged architecture reflected in the original barriers, stonework, and barrels. In a place where every element of the design was created with giving guests the *Frozen* experience, the plastic diluted the quality of the design work and therefore the immersion. Switchbacks and winding lines are common, but that is why the surrounding areas are so highly staged, to help entertain and distract. The aesthetically dissonant barriers, and the muddied visuals they create, serve as a reminder of being penned in and confined, emphasizing the waiting and all the elements that look, for want of a better word, more magical without the barrier.

EMPTINESS: INDIANA JONES EPIC STUNT SPECTACULAR AND PROJECT TOMORROW

The plastic dividers are an obvious example of a visible-invisible barrier: they are clear and therefore trying to be invisible, but draw attention to their presence, making them visi-

---

19 This paper uses were/are because in December 2021, many of these indoor line barriers were still in place, and given the unpredictable, still-developing nature of COVID, it is uncertain what modifications remain or may be reinstated at any given time for the foreseeable future.

ble, and of course they are literally a barrier. They hopefully block COVID transmission, and they block sightlines, which in turn block/impede visitors' ability to engage in the WDW fantasy. The social distancing markings work in a similar way. The parks rerouted and reformed pathways and open areas and emptied out theatrical stages altogether. Throughout the parks, fully immersive, themed spaces became either areas guests could not occupy or unthemed rest areas where people could spread out. These empty spaces, invisible in the sense that they are outdoor, open-aired parts of the parks, draw attention to themselves because they are so still and quiet, lacking the usual lively entertainment.

Emptiness was perhaps the most abstract phenomenon, and not something typically associated with theme park spaces. In a place that is always full of visitors, WDW has a space issue, in that there few empty, cool, or shaded areas. Outside spaces are staged to fulfill the demands of narrative immersion while also maintaining guest traffic flow, so the park design forgoes an abundance of benches and seating in favor of wide, themed walkways or special theatrical detailing, such as the speakers, lighting, and alien plants in Animal Kingdom's Pandora: World of Avatar. Parks also want and need guests to move. Guests are consumers, and park design encourages consuming as much Disney realism and merchandise as possible. The best way to stay cool in the Florida parks is to stay moving or go to events, stores, or eateries, where there is often shade and fans or air conditioning. During first wave COVID protocols, however, the stage shows stopped, which created a lot of unused empty stages and audience seating. Stage spaces like Hollywood Studios' Indiana Jones Epic Stunt Spectacular stopped all showings and became socially distanced seating areas for guests, euphemistically named "relaxation stations" (see Fig. 5). Relaxing in the parks is almost a misnomer, as guests run from ride to ride or from scheduled event to event. The relaxation station sign, on an unthemed plastic sandwich board, is a stark present consciousness reminder negating the Indiana Jones staging. The carefully selected typeface, rope-wrapped beams and poles, and the camouflaged canopy enhance guest narrative immersion when seeing the stunt show. Without the stunt show, and with the COVID reminders, the theatrical staging highlights what is absent.

The Indiana Jones Epic Stunt Spectacular was just unused performance space, unlit and unoccupied, with markings of what once was there. Outside the theatre, there was a huge sign that read "Production Schedule," usually listing daily show times. In May 2021, the sign had a permanent "Production Schedule: No Performances Today" listing. A similar permanent absence was visible just to the left of the auditorium, with an Indiana Jones Stunt Show store that said "Sorry, we're closed." Sitting in this area meant processing a COVID reality instead of experiencing or crafting a Disney reality. The empty stage space in the moment acted as a quiet break from the density of a theme park day, with all its consistent movement and sensory overload. A break like that is rare and pleasant in the middle of a Disney park trip. However, a major element of these areas was unused theatricality. The auditorium itself was awash with stage equipment, stage manager booth, trap doors, and empty vehicles. The emptiness foregrounds the impossibility of indulging in fantasy narratives and mythic time without theatricality. All around the relaxation station were reminders of what was not there: unfulfilled spectacle with literally no spectacular stunts, unfulfilled immersion in the action, and unfulfilled nostalgia for the film. This idea of going unfulfilled is what Disney was fighting against, and arguably losing to, in the shifts to limiting experiences.

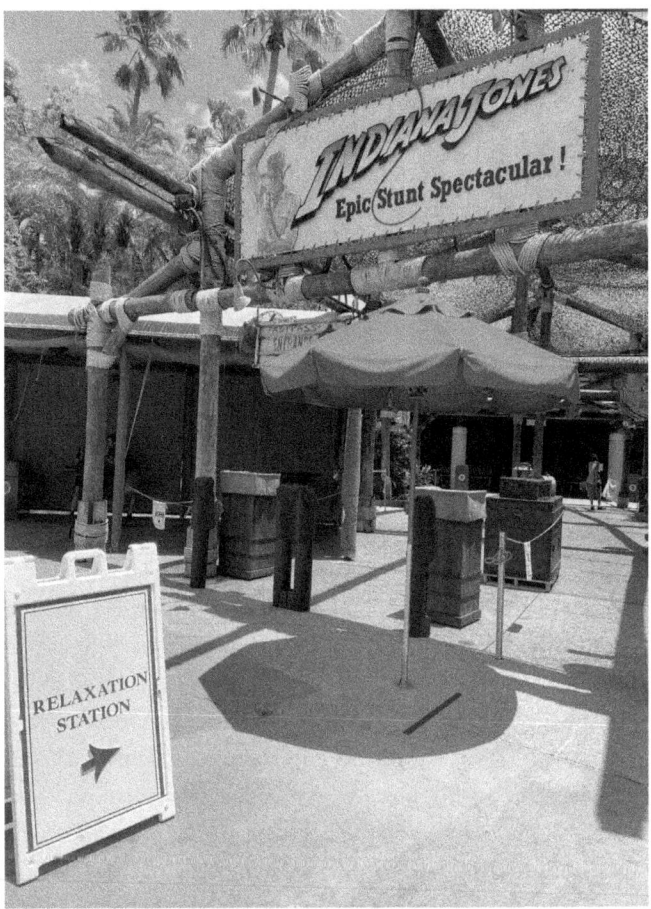

FIG. 5: A Relaxation Station in Hollywood Studios, formerly
the seating area for The Indiana Jones Epic Stunt Spectacular,
May 2021 (photo by author)

The emptiness in the Indiana Jones theatre space is something visitors must seek out to experience. The stage area,
like others in the WDW parks, is tucked away for traffic flow.
A theatrical stage, like the shutdown Fantasmic! or Festi-
val of the Lion King or the stunt show, needs a huge spatial
footprint to produce shows and house audiences, so they are

more readily cordoned off or ignorable than other areas of emptiness in the COVID-adjusted parks. The park redesign also required active discouragement of immersion and play for the operational attractions and rides, not just shuttering stage shows. The carefully crafted and themed spaces within WDW ride lines are key to entertaining, fascinating, and immersing visitors who are waiting for rides. The interactivity helps with the mythic time that crafts ride narratives and distracts from the reality of long lines, hot weather, and crowded park areas. Space is most at a premium in ride lines, and the use of highly sculpted staging and narrative playthings help maximize guest distraction.

Concern over lack of line entertainment, in something like Magic Kingdom's The Many Adventures of Winnie the Pooh ride lines, might seem a bit precious, but the lack of access and empty spaces highlight unfulfillment—precisely the quality that WDW world seeks to avoid. In the line up to the Winnie the Pooh ride, there are many activities to interact with. The target audience for the ride skews toward younger children, so having entertainment helps with impatience. But again, interactivity leads to narrative play and fantasy realism. Pulling up Rabbit's garden or spreading the honey on the digital honey wall heightens the immersion into Pooh's world, the spectacle of the experience,[20] and the nostalgia for Milne's characters, as guests tramp through the

---

20 There is a large multi-sided digital wall in the queue, filled with the image of dripping honey. Set in the pages of a book as a kind of living storybook, the wall is tactical and visceral. The look of the digital honey is goopy and thick, and it is very pleasing to move around by touching the screen. The more guests wipe the screens, the more of the book reveals itself, with images of Pooh and friends. Guests in fact must wipe the screens to reveal the imagery under the honey. It is a high tech and engaging part of the queue line, but communal with a lot of hands touching the screens at the same time.

Hundred Acre Woods. Instead of interactivity, these spaces were roped off and empty. Guests moved through these interactive staged spaces, with touchable, playable elements, all with signs that read "FOR YOUR SAFETY NOT AVAILABLE." The signage, like the Relaxation Station sign, shifted focus from a magical illusion to COVID reality. Also, like the Relaxation Station, the sign implies not touching is for the benefit of guests. The sign indicates that Disney as a company is keeping guests healthy as well as keeping parks open. As guests did not, because they could not, enter and embody the Hundred Acre Woods, guests instead notice the actual lack of bodies at play and the emptiness around play structures.

Emptiness might be the most intuitive, and certainly the most apparent, visible-invisible barrier, as the Project Tomorrow figures (Fig. 6, 7) clarify. Everyone walked directly to the exit after EPCOT's Spaceship Earth rather than exploring around Project Tomorrow. There was no direct messaging about what guests could and could not do after the ride, outside of cast members' general gesture for people to move off the ride and into the large room full of imaginary ideas for the future that encompasses Project Tomorrow. In a room traditionally full of sounds, screens, and interactive stations, everything was quiet and empty. It was implied that everyone should walk out. Stepping out of line to photograph the area was perfectly acceptable, but just not something to do, so very few people did. In part, guests did not stop because there was nothing to photograph. All the interactive screens were blank, eliminating play. The "Energy" part of the room, consisting of large digital shuffle boards, was being used as storage for chairs. The emptiness was palpable; standing around looking at blank screens and social distance seating felt intrusive. To stay was to break with some unstated COVID social convention within the parks, the visible line of people exiting and invisible lack of anyone staying and exploring. It was a lonely, uninviting place, which is the opposite of how people imagine WDW and how Disney advertises its parks.

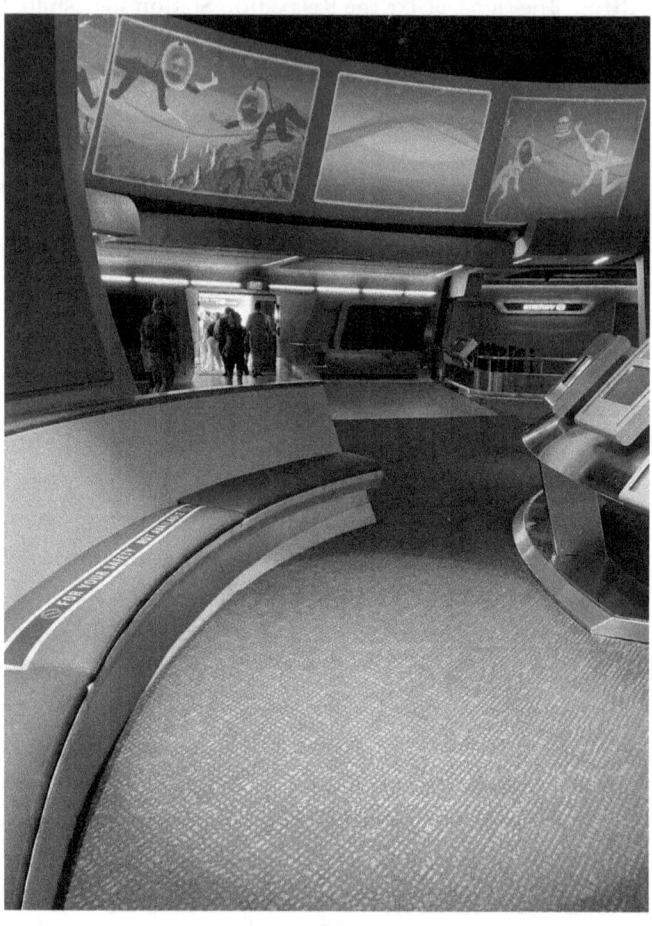

FIG. 6: Project Tomorrow exiting Spaceship Earth,
May 2021 (photo by author)

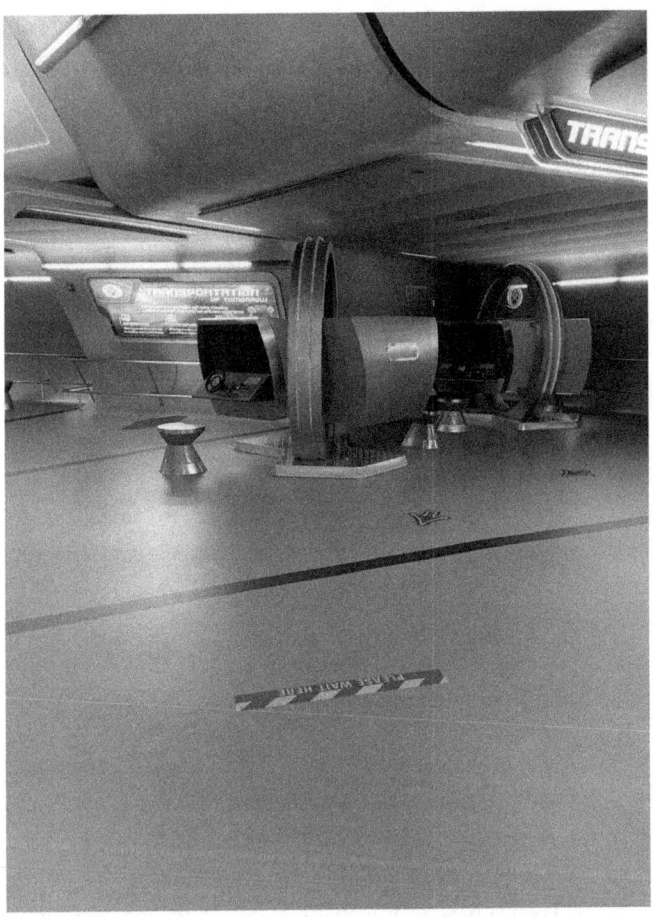

FIG. 7: Project Tomorrow exiting Spaceship Earth,
May 2021 (photo by author)

CONCLUSION: UNFULFILLED NARRATIVES

The implications of the COVID changes mean the Disney parks, as a place marketed to wish fulfillment and fantasy becoming reality, was not really providing that experience during 2021. The COVID protocols translated to limitations, "cannots" and "for your safety, do nots," in place of open exploration and purchase of fantasy. In May 2021, guests could not just walk into stores; there were cast members doing head counts. Guests could not sit and watch a parade because there were no parades. They could not talk with and hug their favorite characters or enroll kids in the Jedi training academy. Again, the COVID safety protocols set in place helped the health of employees and guests. They were important restructurings that also created constant reminders of real-world traumas, crises, and problems. Returning to Koren-Kuik's idea in the epigraph, if "parks are true enclaves of the imaginary where cares of the outside world are temporarily put aside and forgotten," then the COVID additions and changes mean the outside world cannot be put aside. For some fans and guests, park going is central to their engagement with popular culture or immersion with intellectual property, and they invest time, energy, and money into these enclaves of the imaginary. The reminders and signals of the outside world meant an inability for guests to find mythic time or fulfill themed invitations.

In attempting to give some level of exhibition, fantasy, and magic during COVID, Disney inadvertently gave audiences reminders of all these cannots, leading to a lack of immersive, spectacular, or nostalgic fulfillment. Consider the cavalcades. The WDW Prep School website states "cavalcades are kind of like a mini parade. They typically have one float and some characters" ("Complete Guide"). During the day in Magic Kingdom, masked cast members cleared small areas of Main Street and Frontierland for these small cavalcades like Tinkerbell riding a treasure chest, which is one float from previous parades. Tinkerbell alone on a treasure chest is a hint of the spectacular, with the size and artistry of the float. It is a reminder that Tinkerbell, like other mainstay characters, is part of the Magic Kingdom fantasy. But it is mostly a reminder of previous experiences. This treasure chest float is actually part of many Magic Kingdom parades, including one part of the huge (and hugely popular) Mickey's Not So Scary Halloween Boo to You parade. Her isolation, as one parade float on its own, highlights what's missing: huge shows, a variety of entertainments, and Tinkerbell flying over Main Street during fireworks. Here she is, in broad daylight, a piece of nostalgia for what's currently missing in the parks.

WORKS CITED

Beeton, Sue. *Film-Induced Tourism.* Channel View Publications, 2016.

"Complete Guide to Characters and Cavalcades in EPCOT." WDWPrepSchool, https://wdwprepschool.com/disney -world-parks/epcot/characters-cavalcades/. Accessed June 27, 2022.

Freitag, Florian. "The 'Politics of Inclusion/Exclusion' in Times of the Pandemic." *Journal of Themed Experience and Attractions Studies:* 2.1 (2022), 13-16.

Kaitlyn & Skylar Dickerson [@thenottwintwins]. "Today is the one, the only" Photo of users and Ariel. Instagram, 17 Nov. 2021, https://www.instagram.com/p/CWYr7uyrs mq/.

Kokai, Jennifer A. and Robson, Tom. "Disney during COVID-19: The tourist and the actor's nightmare," *Journal of Themed Experience and Attractions Studies:* 2.1 (2022), 17-20.

Koren-Kuik, Meyrav. "Desiring the Tangible: Disneyland, Fandom and Spatial Immersion." Fan *CULTure: Essays on*

Participatory Fandom in the 21st Century, edited by Jonathan Malcolm Lampley and Kristin M. Barton, McFarland, 2013, 146-158.

Lantz, Victoria Pettersen. "Reimagineering Tourism: Tourist-Performer Style at Disney's Dapper Days." *The Journal of Popular Culture:* 52.6 (2019), 1334-1354.

Lukas, Scott A. "Introduction." *A Reader in Themed and Immersive Spaces,* edited by Scott A. Lukas. ETC Press, 2016, 3-18.

———. "Theming as a Sensory Phenomenon: Discovering the Senses on the Las Vegas Strip." *The Themed Space: Locating Culture, Nation, and Self,* edited by Scott A. Lukas. Lexington Books, 2007, 75-96.

"Meet Ariel at Her Grotto." Walt Disney World, https://disneyworld.disney.go.com/entertainment/magic-king dom/character-meet-ariel-grotto-fantasyland/. Accessed April 4, 2022.

Mist the Mermaid [@mistthemermaid]. "Happy #throwbackthursday!" Photo of user and Ariel. Instagram, 27 Jan. 2022, https://www.instagram.com/p/CZPN9ANr wSK/.

Smith, Matthew Wilson. "Bayreuth, Disneyland, and the Return to Nature." *Land/Scape/Theater,* edited by Elinor Fuchs and Una Chaudhuri, University of Michigan Press, 2002, 252-279.

"Tam Tam Drummers of Harambe." Walt Disney World, https://disneyworld.disney.go.com/entertainment/animal-kingdom/tam-tam-congo/. Accessed August 15, 2022.

Turner, Sarah E. "Blackness, Bayous and Gumbo: Encoding and Decoding Race in a Colorblind World." *Diversity in Disney Films: Critical Essays on Race, Ethnicity, Gender, Sexuality and Disability,* edited by Johnson Cheu, McFarland, 2013, 83-97.

Wallace, Michael. *Mickey Mouse History and Other Essays on American Memory.* Temple University Press, 1996.

Waysdorf, Abby E. *Fan Sites: Film Tourism and Contemporary Fandom.* University of Iowa Press, 2021.

Weaver, David. *Sustainable Tourism.* Taylor & Francis, 2007.

Williams, Rebecca. *Theme Park Fandom: Spatial Transmedia, Materiality and Participatory Cultures.* Amsterdam University Press, 2020.

"Alternate Universe – No COVID-19": Fanfiction and Cultural Trauma

By Sarah Breyfogle

ABSTRACT

Using cultural trauma theory and literary trauma theory, this paper examines how fanfiction writers used ficwriting to explore pandemic trauma. It conducts a textual analysis of five fics that center their plot around some aspect of COVID-19 precautions and restrictions. This research finds that the authors demonstrate community care; that they self-disclose that they or others they know are struggling; and that actual infection, illness, or death are rarely presented within the fics.

Keywords: fanfiction, fan culture, COVID-19, Star Wars

"Universo Alterno – Sin COVID-19": *Fanfiction* y Trauma Cultural

RESUMEN

Al utilizar la teoría del trauma cultural y la teoría del trauma literario, este artículo examina cómo los escritores de *fanfiction* utilizaron la escritura de ficción para explorar el trauma pandémico. Realiza un análisis textual de cinco ficciones que centran su trama en algún aspecto de las precauciones y restricciones del COVID-19. Esta investigación encuentra que los autores demuestran cuidado comunitario; que ellos mismos revelan que ellos u otros que conocen están luchando; y que la infección, la enfermedad o la muerte reales rara vez se presentan en las ficciones.

Palabras clave: *fanfiction*, cultura de fans, COVID-19, Star Wars

"平行世界——没有COVID-19"：同人小说与文化创伤

摘要：本文运用文化创伤理论和文学创伤理论，分析了同人小说作家如何通过小说写作来探索大流行创伤。本文对五部小说进行了文本分析，这些小说的情节围绕2019冠状病毒病（COVID-19）预防和限制措施的某些方面展开。本研究发现，小说作者展示了社区关怀；他们自我披露称其或其认识的人正在苦苦挣扎；真实的感染、疾病或死亡很少出现在小说中。

关键词：同人小说，同人文化，2019冠状病毒病，《星球大战》

Beginning in March of 2020, people around the world experienced a profound disruption to their way of life, in many cases overnight, as COVID-19 lockdowns proliferated. To help cope with the uncertainty and fear of the pandemic, many people found themselves turning to media in an attempt to escape from or moderate that disruption. For fans, particularly those already invested in creative enterprises around fandom, media had already been a central part of their lives. While it is likely that some fan creators felt their desire to participate in their earlier fan activities diminish, many others, trapped at home with little else enjoyable to occupy their time, found an outlet to express their love of their particular texts as a response to the stress of the pandemic.

The link between the pandemic and transformative fan works is particularly apparent on the popular fanfiction hosting website and nonprofit Archive of Our Own (often abbrevi-

ated to Ao3). Ao3's extensive searching and database func-
tionality allows for the tagging of fanfiction's wide variety of
tropes that can be utilized to encourage the development of
romantic—and, less frequently, platonic—relationships between characters in a practice called shipping. Popular tropes
include being snowed in together; staying at an inn or hotel
that only has one bed available; and one character taking care
of another while they are sick. It is not surprising, then, that
the altered life practices adopted during the pandemic offer
fertile ground to the enterprising fanfiction writer. For the
purposes of this paper, fanfiction, fanfic, and fic will be used
interchangeably to refer to the same form of transformative
fictional texts.

To easily identify conventions within fanfiction, a large fandom is necessary, and as such this analysis focuses on *Star
Wars* fandom's most popular ship; Kylo Ren and Rey, often
abbreviated to Reylo. Within the body of fanfiction that has
been written about the pairing, a meaningful number of fics
have been written that place the two characters and their romantic development within the present-day COVID-19 pandemic. Exploring the conventions of these fics illuminates
how fanfiction writers have used fanfiction to cope with their
pandemic experiences.

Cultural and literary trauma theory provides an avenue to
examine this phenomenon, using as texts five Reylo fanfics
that center their plot around the changes to everyday life that
occurred as a result of the COVID-19 pandemic. Following
on previous scholars' practices of close textual analysis of fan
works (Kaplan; Leavenworth; Black et al.), these fics provide
an avenue to examine how fanfiction expresses the strains
and upheavals of the unprecedented pandemic and how the
practice of sharing those experiences through publicly post-

201

ed fanfiction operates to express and alleviate the shared trauma of both authors and readers.

UNDERSTANDING FANS AND FANFICTION

To write about fans, it becomes crucial to define what a fan is; however, such definitions are fraught. Duffet's 2013 definition provides a helpful starting point; that "media fandom is the recognition of a positive, personal, relatively deep, emotional connection with a mediated element of popular culture" (Duffet 2). However, what is crucially absent from this definition is that people form social connections because of their shared emotional connection to a piece of media, and that this shared communal connection creates vibrant communities. These communities discuss their chosen piece of media; they create fanfiction and fan art that reimagines the world of the story; they may even create and share physical items such as plushies or knitting patterns. Drawing a hard line between who is a fan and who is simply a casual enjoyer of a piece of media is unnecessary and unhelpful, but it is important to acknowledge that people experience fandom on a continuum, from a deep emotional connection so powerful that it motivates someone to get a tattoo related to their fandom to a quiet enjoyment found rewatching a comforting show.

Furthermore, during the COVID-19 pandemic, the framing of this emotional connection shifted. Hoyeck notes that the narrative around binge-watching multiple episodes, seasons, or shows became much more positive and guilt-free; furthermore, she highlights that the social capital created by knowing a piece of media extremely well helps to stave off feelings of isolation (Hoyeck 36). The boundaries around who qualifies as "fan enough" have never been particularly impermeable; however, the pandemic has undeniably made them even more porous. Therefore, this analysis is more concerned with how people enact fandom; specifically, through the writing and reading of fanfiction.

Henry Jenkins' seminal work, *Textual Poachers*, situates fanfiction as a form "of cultural production characteristic of fandom" (Jenkins 159). By contrast, Coppa describes fanfiction as something experienced in a gendered way (Coppa xii). For Coppa, fanfiction is not just about the cultural object, but about the experience of consuming the object—and, in fact, consuming multiple instances of the object, similar to eating an entire sleeve of Oreos. Still, she does offer some definition of the fanfiction itself, arguing that fanfiction is a collection of fiction created outside the traditional publishing industry, which rewrites and transforms existing stories created by others while following the conventions of a particular fan community.

What is crucial is that these stories are shared within, indeed often used to create, a community. Jenkins describes a group of women getting together to write fanzines in one of their homes; De Kosnik argues in her critique of *Fifty Shades of Grey* that bodies of fanfiction work are archives of women's culture. That this community is predominantly women is taken as the basis of analysis for many examinations of fanfiction, although people of all genders write fanfic. Furthermore, because fanfiction is typically derivative of copyrighted media, it usually cannot be legally bought or sold. The result is what Hellekson describes as a "gift economy, not a commercial one" (Hellekson 114). This process of exchange, as mediated by a series of conventions and names for practices that serve as an in-group-out-group boundary, reinforces the strength of the fanfiction writing community. Fan art, fan edits, and other forms of fan creation also circulate within this community.

The fanfiction being exchanged can take many forms. Fanfiction can vary in length, ranging from 100-word drabbles to 500,000-word monoliths—and, in notable instances, even longer.[1] Some fanfics attempt to remain close to the original story, describing themselves as "canon compliant"—or, in some places, "canon complicit," implying a connection to some nefarious event in canon such as the death of a beloved character or an unpopular narrative choice. Others take place in alternate universes, or AUs. Fanfics are also organized by tropes, ranging from the general, such as hurt/comfort, angst, or fluff, to the specific and sexually explicit, such as omegaverse or mpreg.[2] Fics can combine content from multiple sources into crossover fics or introduce extensive original characters (OCs). Importantly, these categories are coherent to the community of fans who read them. As Coppa notes, "fanfiction is written within and for particular communities that have highly specific expectations for fiction, which can be seen in their elaborate vocabulary and critical literature" (Coppa 9).

These fics have likewise been stored in a myriad of places. Jenkins discusses zines, "photocopied anthologies of short stories, poems, and artwork centering on one or more media 'universes' and written by multiple authors" (Jenkins 160). While zines are occasionally still produced, with the rise of the internet, fanfiction tended to move online to sites like LiveJournal and fanfiction.net. However, rules around internet pornography—particularly gay pornography—resulted in a series of shutdowns and deletions that alarmed and angered fans (Brennan). The call came for a platform where fans owned the servers and so in 2008 Archive of Our Own was developed as an open-source, fan-built and coded non-profit.

ARCHIVE OF OUR OWN AND THE PARATEXTS
OF FANFICTION

Ao3 is notable for several reasons. First, it is "a community of mostly women, who are traditionally underrepresented in computer science and even more so in open-source development"; second, "they didn't just build a platform; they also built a batch of fan-coders because, as the founders realized at the time: 'we're going to have to grow our own'" (Fiesler n.p.). However, even more interesting than its origin is the robust tagging system that has been developed, maintained by volunteers called "tag-wranglers" who "wrangle" the individual tags, ensuring that despite different permutations of the tag, a coherent set emerges. An example of this is when a ship is indicated with both a slash, such as Kirk/Spock, Spock/Kirk, and ship name Spirk. A tag wrangler ensures that all three permutations are considered the same by the site. A tag that has not had this process done to it is considered freeform; some freeform tags are later wrangled, while others remain freeform. A tag considered to be in the process of wrangling, or will be wrangled soon, is called an "unwrangled" tag. This tagging system is a form of "curated folksonomy" (Bullard) that combines self-expression through tags with an organizational system to rival library databases. Because of its robustness, it is extremely useful for examining specific types of fanfictions.

When scholars have attempted to analyze fanfiction writers, rather than what is presented in their fics, they often utilize these paratexts. Leavenworth analyzes author's notes on one multi-chapter fic from a narrative perspective, examining how the author develops a relationship with her readers and shares aspects of her personal life. Black et al. focus on communally shared identity, specifically the author's self-identification with the autistic community while writing fanfiction in which a character is reimagined as autistic. Both studies utilize such paratexts to determine significant things about the author; this study does the same. This allows at least tentative conclusions to be drawn about the writer without simply and often unfairly extrapolating from their works of fiction.

Freeform: Covid 19 AU (1)

Freeform: Covid 19 be like (1)

Freeform: Covid 19 content (2)

Freeform: Covid 19 doesn't exist (1)

Freeform: covid 19 doesn't exist lol (1)

Freeform: covid 19 fic (3)

Freeform: covid 19 got me like (1)

Freeform: COVID 19 implied (1)

Freeform: COVID 19 Influenced (1)

Freeform: COVID 19 IS A BITCH (1)

Freeform: covid 19 is a thing in this fic btw lmao (1)

Freeform: Covid 19 lockdown (1)

Freeform: COVID 19 mention (2)

Freeform: Covid 19 never happened (1)

Fig. 1. A selection of tags on fanfiction website Archive of Our Own relating to COVID-19.

One currently "unwrangled" tag is the COVID-19 tag (Fig. 1), which had 393 variations as of November 2021. Taken together, these tags read almost as a community-created poem where the impact of the pandemic is rejected, accepted, raged against, or used as a creative tool all at the same time (Fig. 1). However, because of this variance, the category had to be refined further to one pairing popular enough to ensure a wide selection of fics that included both the pairing and a COVID-19 element.

REYLO FANFICTION

Specifically, this paper examines fics that explore the relationship between Rey and villain-turned-anti-hero Kylo Ren, as developed in the *Star Wars* sequel trilogy that began in 2015 with *Star Wars: Episode VII – The Force Awakens* and concluded with *Star Wars: Episode IX – The Rise of Skywalker* in 2019. The pairing, often abbreviated to "Reylo" in line with the fannish tradition of combining two characters' names to give them a "ship name," has been the source of much discussion online within academic and fan communities—and their overlap. Hoffman provides an in-depth analysis of the second film's portrayal of Kylo Ren as a sympathetic yet ultimately blameworthy character, while Busse highlights the divisiveness of the pairing within fan discussions:

> In *The Force Awakens* fandom, for example, there is a vocal contingent of anti-Reylo fans, that is, fans who hate Rey/Kylo, the pairing of the main female character and the main male villain in the latest Star Wars movie. Anti-Reylos read the pairing's on-screen encounters as rape, and they point out the age difference and potential famil-

ial relationship. Often declaring themselves younger or even underage, with many self-defining as childhood abuse survivors, anti-Reylos not only hate the pairing but find its very existence triggering. Calling Reylo fans abusive and pedophiles, in turn, causes Reylo fans to become nasty, often each side spamming the other with their vitriol. (Busse n.p.).

This conflict is important to acknowledge as context for the COVID-19 fics, which do not represent the concerns presented by anti-fans of the pairing. In accordance with the traditional fandom practice of "not yucking another's yum," this pairing is examined, in this context, as a transformative reading distinct from what is portrayed on-screen. Certainly, the authors are not writing for the anti-fans; furthermore, all fics examined were tagged as "fluff," which implies the avoidance of dark topics in favor of sweeter and more comforting content. The controversial nature of the pairing as it is presented on-screen, as well as fans' legitimate responses to it, serve to highlight the truly transformative nature of these fics.

The controversial nature of the pairing provides a window into the dangers of extrapolating too heavily about fanfiction writers based solely on the nature of their writing. It would be inappropriate to argue that all Reylo shippers would see no issue with a real-world man acting as Kylo Ren does; it would be equally inappropriate to argue that the pairing is not reflective of patriarchal structures that privilege the forgiveness of white men in even egregious circumstances. Coker and Viars provide a thorough discussion of this issue, although their article must be qualified because it was completed before the Rey/Kylo Ren pairing was canonized in *The Rise of Skywalker*.

CULTURAL TRAUMA THEORY AND LITERARY TRAUMA THEORY

These texts and paratexts are analyzed from the perspective of cultural trauma theory. Alexander (2004) succinctly defines cultural trauma as a situation in which "members of a collectivity feel they have been subjected to a horrendous event that leaves indelible marks upon their group consciousness, marking their memories forever and changing their future identity in fundamental and irrevocable ways" (Alexander 1). It is easy to argue that the COVID-19 pandemic has been a traumatic event that has impacted people collectively. However, what Alexander further elucidates is that traumatic events must be assigned meaning as traumatic by a collective to move into the realm of cultural trauma. The important element then becomes not the actual conditions of the trauma—in this case, the pandemic—but how meaning is created from those conditions and shared within a community.

Because this research is not concerned with all forms of meaning creation, literary trauma theory serves as a secondary theory; specifically, Pederson's 2014 revision is used. Pederson argues that literary trauma theory must catch up to the science of trauma and recognize that people who have experienced traumatic events are not only capable of constructing coherent, reliable accounts of those events, but also that the re-construction of those events can be cathartic and healing (Pederson 338). This understanding of literary trauma theory is, however, concerned with the individual who has experienced trauma; cultural trauma theory provides a way of examining how trauma functions across a creative community. Taken together, these two theories provide a way of understanding how fanfiction writers make sense of their individual experiences of a collectively shared trauma, within the context of established fandoms and ficwriter communities.

From this perspective, two research questions emerge: how do fanfic writers on Ao3 express their experiences with the COVID-19 pandemic, both creatively and factually? And, as a secondary question: how do fanfic writers engage in communal practices of trauma articulation and healing?

METHOD

Fics were selected based on a combination of factors. The first is that they all share the same pairing –a romantic relationship between *Star Wars* characters Kylo Ren and Rey. This pairing was selected based on the size of the fandom and the popularity of the pairing, which resulted in a significant number of fics and allowed other factors to be held constant. Second, fics were short enough to be manageable. Third, the fics explored the everyday experiences of living through a pandemic, rather than placing the plot in a more dramatic setting that the author likely did not have personal experience with. Fourth, fics were selected based on quality, popularity, and completeness, with well-written and reviewed fics being preferred over fics with poorer writing or less engagement. Incomplete fics were not considered. Finally, while many fanfics include extensive sex scenes, all fics selected were rated M or lower to ensure that the focus remained on the impact of the pandemic on daily life, not on the possibilities it provided for erotic potential.[3]

Fics were examined through close textual analysis and its associated paratexts—title, author notes, and tags (see Fig. 2). Fics were read initially for appropriateness to the topic, then read again and annotated for preliminary coding. Fics were then re-read as needed to identify themes.

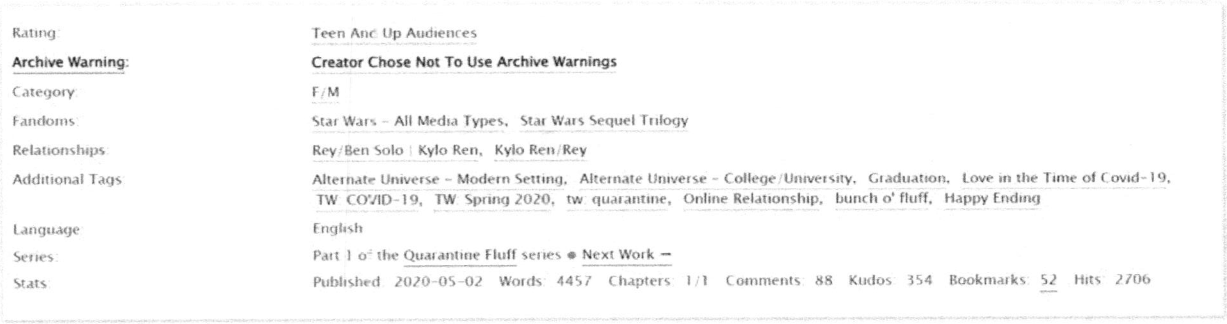

Rating	Teen And Up Audiences
Archive Warning:	**Creator Chose Not To Use Archive Warnings**
Category	F/M
Fandoms	Star Wars – All Media Types, Star Wars Sequel Trilogy
Relationships	Rey/Ben Solo | Kylo Ren, Kylo Ren/Rey
Additional Tags	Alternate Universe – Modern Setting, Alternate Universe – College/University, Graduation, Love in the Time of Covid-19, TW COVID-19, TW Spring 2020, tw quarantine, Online Relationship, bunch o' fluff, Happy Ending
Language	English
Series	Part 1 of the Quarantine Fluff series ⬤ Next Work →
Stats	Published 2020-05-02 Words 4457 Chapters 1/1 Comments 88 Kudos 354 Bookmarks 52 Hits 2706

Fig. 2: The interface presented to a user at the top of each fanfic. This interface describes Fic 2, "Pomp Under the Circumstances."

ABOUT THE FICS

All five fics were categorized as "fluff" or some variation and included the well-established tag "Alternate Universe – Modern Setting." There were no attempts to place the pandemic within the *Star Wars* setting. Each fic included a tag about its COVID-19 material and three of them couched the tag in "warning" or "tw," short for trigger warning, indicating an awareness of trauma responses around the subject. The fics were all published in 2020, between April and August of that year. Each author provided a brief author's note; one indicated that the project was a collaboration and shared the authors' Twitter handles, while the rest offered some commentary on the fic. Two author's notes provided an additional trigger warning for COVID-19 content, while a third exhorted readers to "stay home as much as you can, cousins. It's dangerous out there" (VR_Trakowski). A fourth described the story as an "and they were zoommates" fic, in reference to the meme from now-defunct video sharing platform Vine, "and they were roommates"; the reference served as a playful way of indicating the premise of the fic. In addition, all fics referred to Ben Solo, the birth name of the son of Han Solo and Princess Leia, rather than Kylo Ren, the name that the character took on after falling to the Dark Side. This naming convention indicates an attachment to the potential of Ben Solo as a maladjusted but ultimately kind young man, rather than the neo-fascist persona of Kylo Ren.

Fics are analyzed below in order from shortest to longest in terms of word count. All titles retain their original capitalization, as non-normative capitalization strategies serve as stylistic indicators.

Fic 1: *"you are the best thing that's ever been mine"*

The first fic, published in August of 2020, is the shortest. The author discloses through their author's notes that they wrote the fic to help cope with being separated from their boyfriend of four years, and that some scenes in the fic are correspondingly autobiographical. The fic is organized through a series of flashbacks from Rey's perspective. Rey is cast as a recent college grad waiting to see her boyfriend, Ben Solo, who has finally managed to book a flight to see her post-lockdown. Her impatience is highlighted by moving between brief scenes of her restlessness and chronological vignettes of their established relationship. When the pandemic interrupts these flashbacks, the scenes become memories of Zoom conversations rather than in-person ones.

Fic 2: *"Pomp Under the Circumstances"*

In this fic, Rey is cast as a former foster kid and college student preparing to graduate when the pandemic hits. Ben is a teaching assistant assigned to her course. During lockdown, they develop a friendship and then a relationship. Large portions of the fic take an epistolic form, detailing text conversations between the two. One other franchise character makes an appearance: Luke Skywalker as the provost of the university, who, at Ben's request, holds a virtual graduation ceremony for Rey. The fic concludes with Rey getting a chance to walk at her graduation the following year once restrictions are lifted. The fic is dedicated to a friend "who deserves all the pomp and circumstance." We may that the friend was in Rey's situation, unable to walk at graduation, due to the pandemic and that the gift of the fic was intended to help alleviate the blow.

Fic 3: "The New Normal"

This fic explores the relationship that develops between Rey and her attractive next-door neighbor Ben during lockdown as they both work from home at their desks near opposite windows. Again, the fic takes on an epistolic form; the characters start by writing notes and holding them up to their respective windows, before progressing to phone and video conversations and occasional in-person, albeit appropriately distanced, dates. This fic is longer and rated M rather than T, which means that aspects of digital intimacy through text and video call are alluded to as well. As in the previous fics, the story ends with an in-person meeting as the restrictions lift.

Fic 4: "the one I have been waiting for"

This fic has the most elaborate premise; Rey is an author and Ben is the editor assigned to work with her during lockdown. The fic significantly incorporates other characters from the franchise; family relationships remain intact, with Leia serving as the owner of the publishing firm and Finn and Poe as Rey's friends. These other characters are, by and large, in happy relationships regardless of their canon status; Finn and Poe are implied to be in a relationship, while Ben's family is reimagined as a happy, if chaotic, one that has family dinners via Zoom, with Han and Leia still married and Chewbacca portrayed as an eccentric uncle. Ben and Rey's relationship develops within the context of this meddling family in multiple points. Like previous fics, emails and groupchats feature prominently. The eventual in-person meet-up does not conclude the fic; instead, the characters quarantine prior to meeting up. The conclusion, however, is the removal of restrictions; the characters are able to get ice cream, albeit with a reservation to ensure limited capacity at the ice cream parlor.

Fic 5: *"A House Turned Upside Down"*

This fic is the longest; Ben is cast as the somewhat estranged child of divorced parents Han and Leia. While grocery shopping on behalf of his parents out of concern for their health, he develops a crush on grocery store clerk Rey. This fic is also darker, while still warranting a fluff tag; Rey's difficulties as an essential worker during the pandemic and Ben's struggles to figure out how to handle his familial obligations are both crucial elements of the story. The fic hinges on a case of unknown identity; Ben cannot find Rey after she loses her job due to a non-COVID illness, until a chance encounter reunites them. Masks compound the issue, as neither of them know what the other looks like without a mask. This fic features the most in-person socialization, with the two conversing on Rey's front porch and hugging at the end of their conversations. As time passes, the weather becomes a concern for socializing, and that combined with lowering cases move their conversations inside, where they progress to a full-fledged romantic relationship. This fic is unique in that it does not conclude with the lifting of restrictions, only their possibility, and that it infects a character with a disease that is, however briefly, believed by one character to be COVID-19.

MAKING TRAUMA TANGIBLE

Across the fics, paratexts acknowledge that the pandemic was a stressful and traumatic event. Within the fics, the pandemic is demonstrated through the inclusion of physical practices such as mask-wearing, Zoom calls, and ordering food to each other's houses rather than going out to dinner. The longest fic, "A House Turned Upside Down," begins with grocery shopping, which Ben recognizes the instability of: "Things appeared and disappeared in stores at what seemed like random. Getting the next carton of milk before the first was fin-

Did you get it? I got a delivery notification.

A warning would have been nice. I tried to convince the DoorDash guy it wasn't mine, while he kept backing away like I was the COVID monster.

But thank you Ben D

You told me Taco Bell is your favorite.

It sure is. But you could have asked me what I liked instead of buying like the whole menu

But at least now I know why you asked for my address, so I can stop worrying you'll murder me in my sleep

I was worried you'd tell me not to send it.

And I thought that if we were going to watch Galaxy Wars together tonight, it would be nice if we were eating together, too.

You got yourself Taco Bell too??

<Incoming FaceTime call from Ben Solo >

Fig. 3: An epistolic series of text messages between the two characters in "Pomp Under the Circumstances," both representing and describing COVID-19 precautions.

ished was smart." However, almost all the fics end with the conclusion of the pandemic, or at least the lifting of the current restrictions, which provides a sense of resolution to both the relationship and the characters' struggles.

Many fics also utilize epistolic conventions, directly reproducing text conversations and emails into the fic; one even includes a subtle joke about the signatures that bookend each email. These texts and emails often increase the visceral feeling of isolation, with characters describing what they would do if they could only meet in person. Loneliness is a common theme, in the context of missing a partner but also in the context of the pandemic. In "the one I have been waiting for," Rey finds herself early for a work meeting; "being early had never been one of her defining characteristics, but she also hadn't had any real human interaction in days."

Yearning is a classic romance trope that carries over into fanfiction; however, the yearning and loneliness depicted in the fics has a different dimension because of the overall uncertainty. In "A House Turned Upside Down," it is not simply that Ben cannot find Rey; it is that her absence may be because she is dying from the virus. In "The New Normal," it is not that Rey experiences a mild anxiety disorder and Ben cannot be physically there to reassure her; it is that the pandemic restrictions trigger a response that is undeniably familiar. Contemplating her ongoing self-isolation, Rey thinks that "She was one of the lucky ones. She was still employed. She was healthy. But she was becoming mentally exhausted"—hardly uncommon sentiments as lockdowns dragged on. From the perspective of literary trauma theory, the re-presentation of traumatic events through writing can have a healing effect. Furthermore, because the experiences can be assumed by the author to be familiar to their reader, this re-presentation becomes a communal sharing practice that allows its members to name and process the trauma of the pandemic.

FANFIC AND HEALING

Within paratexts, authors express their own experiences with the pandemic or indicate that their writing is somewhat based on their own experiences. One author writes:

> Since quarantine began I have been in a long-distance relationship with my boyfriend of four years and, well, I haven't been doing so hot because of it. So, one way I've been coping with being apart is writing, and I wanted to compose something with themes from my own relationship.

This author explicitly precedes her fic with the acknowledgment that her fic draws from her own experiences as well as what she imagines for the characters, and that she finds it therapeutic to re-present her own emotions and experiences onto these characters.

This re-presentation is of course of preexisting characters, removed from their canon context and devoid of their special status as Force users and galaxy leaders; what fans would call "comfort characters." Little scholarship has formally defined the existence of a "comfort character," or the fan practice of identifying with a character and magnifying their shared qualities.[4] Characters serve as a point of entry to texts (Gwenllian-Jones), but the process by which fans identify with characters—or, alternatively, find productive differences—remains unclear. The majority of work on fan identification looks at sports fandom, although some scholarship explores melodramatic identification in fiction media fandom.

Schmidt defines melodramatic identification as "a relationship to a continuous interweaving of texts—including both fan fiction and the narrative of the fan herself—into a greater text that the fan knows as 'my show'" (Schmidt, n.p.). This relationship, while appropriate, is too broad to explain the specific identification with a character or a romantic pairing that is present in these fics. Genre conventions offer some insight.

COVID-19 AND SICKFIC

The writers of these selected fics universally steered away from infecting characters in their fics with COVID-19. This is likely in part due to genre conventions; fluff typically deals with light-hearted matter. However, "sickfics," or fics where one character is ill and another must take care of them, certainly can be classified as fluff. Furthermore, fics need not be exclusively one genre; some fics were tagged as "angst and fluff," and a fluff tag may comfortably reside beside a "hurt/ comfort" or "whump" tag. This is demonstrated in Fic 5, which is tagged as "angst and fluff" and includes a character fearing that another has COVID-19—although the character in reality has a common cold and the result is another of many misunderstandings in the fic.

The choice not to give characters COVID-19 must therefore be interpreted as a deliberate decision that goes beyond genre expectations. The analysis of character behaviors and, through author paratexts, writer behaviors indicate widespread caution and anxiety about the pandemic. Infecting a character with a life-threatening virus that remains somewhat mysterious—and at the time that these fics were written, was exceedingly so—could therefore be seen as going "too far" in a way that more familiar illnesses such as the flu or pneumonia would not. Unlike a common cold, which is unpleasant but common and therefore can be turned into writing inspiration, actually contracting COVID-19—particularly in the summer of 2020, when little was known about the virus—would be too terrifying to recount within a few months of the experience. It remains possible that COVID-19 will become a sickfic convention now that vaccines and the loosening of restrictions have changed the narrative around the virus.

This analysis is complicated by the fact that a fluff tag was not a criterion of inclusion. Rather, the five fics selected based on the other, established, criteria were all tagged as fluff, indicating that fluff is a popular genre for COVID-19 fics; the preference for popular fics in the selection criteria is the best indicator of this assertion. It could also be explained by the restriction of fics to those rated M or lower, as lower-rated fics tend to deal with lighter topics. However, plenty of dark topics can be encompassed by an M tag; a lower rating does not necessarily indicate the type of fic. Overall, it seems likely that all fics were tagged as fluff because of the appeal of fluffy, comforting fics that still acknowledged the trauma of the COVID-19 pandemic.

COMMUNITY CARE

It has long been established that fanction is a communal practice, where both pleasure in reading and understanding of what is being read comes from participation in a community (De Kosnik). From these fics, it is apparent that such community participation continues during traumatic events. Some authors even indicated that COVID-19 fics were a trend, implying that they had seen or read other fics like theirs before writing. Community participation was characterized by community care, as indicated by tags and author's notes that referenced trigger warnings as well as by less-standardized exhortations for safety in author's notes.

In the preview of "A House Turned Upside Down," the author writes that "Ben really shouldn't be going out every week, but speaking from my own experience, when you're shopping for three people there's always something someone needs. Stay home as much as you can, cousins. It's dangerous out there" (VR_Trakowski). The usage of "cousins" expresses more intimate care, but other authors express similar sentiments: "Hope very one[sic] is staying safe and healthy" or "Hope everyone is hanging in there!" (krossartist and SuchaPrettyPoison; dawninthemtn). VR_Trakowski also expressed concern that their readers might drink and drive and wanted to reinforce Ben Solo's actions as appropriate for his physical size, indicating that their community concern extended beyond COVID-related care.

The consistent care for the reader indicates an awareness of community; fanfics are written and shared on Ao3 with the assumption and arguably hope that someone will read them. Descriptors like "cousins" indicate the intimate nature of the community. Furthermore, almost all writers are themselves readers, and many readers end up writing. Therefore, while it is possible to speak of a dichotomy between writer and reader in the context of a single fanfic, such a dichotomy is unhelpful when considering the wider community. It is worth noting that this community was also indicated through the understanding on the part of some authors that many other authors were writing quarantine fics: "Everybody's doing quarantine fics, seems like; who am I to resist the trend?", as VR_Trakowski writes. This reinforces the porousness of the boundaries between reader and writer.

CONCLUSION

The findings presented here indicate that fans clearly enjoy reading and writing about a beloved character in an everyday situation and derive comfort from imagining such shared experiences. Such identification may be personal or aspirational, where a writer may feel better able to handle their own experiences if they imagine a beloved and admired character going through the same things. It seems plausible that fics such as those with hurt-comfort or sickfic conventions provide ways of coping with more individualized traumas. A generalized assertion is outside the scope of this paper. Still, within the context of COVID-19 as cultural trauma, these fics demonstrate that the writers and to an extent the readers use fanfiction and identification with fictional characters as a coping mechanism to deal with the pandemic. Writers utilized trigger warnings, statements of compassion, and an awareness of other writers to express community care and desire for readers' safety. Finally, this paper finds support for the idea that quarantine fics are prevalent enough to have some coherent shared meaning amongst fic readers and writers, rather than simply being an anomaly.

The work presented here has some substantial limitations. This paper analyzed fanfictions that *did* explore COVID-19. An equally fruitful analysis could be undertaken of fics that actively expressed that they were *not* including COVID-19 in their modern AU, particularly in terms of what those paratexts expressed. Second, this paper only examined one pairing, and examined fics that were predominantly fluff; an examination of darker genres, such as angst, whump, or hurt/comfort, could reveal radically different conclusions. Finally, fics need not be tagged with any variation of COVID-19, pandemics, or quarantines to still express emotions about those things. Escapism is an equally plausible way of handling trauma, particularly ongoing trauma without a defined end. Identifying the full spectrum of ways that fans have used their fandom to process the trauma of COVID-19 is fascinating and far beyond the scope of this paper. Furthermore, many fans found the stress of the pandemic to limit their ability to participate in fandom, which is its own form of fannish experience with the pandemic that warrants study.

In addition, the focus on modern AUs observed here indicates something about the nature of fan identification, not just with fandoms broadly speaking, but with specific characters within fandom. The ways that fan identification with a character functions may be intuitively familiar to those, like this author, who consider themselves aca-fans. However, more research is certainly needed to identify how such identification is formed; how it functions; and what its effects, both positive and negative, are. Of particular interest is how this identification functions in fics where the beloved character goes through challenging or even torturous experiences as part of the narrative, which can draw compelling connections with scholarship on hurt-comfort and whump fic genres.

The use of modern AUs also provides an interesting snapshot of everyday experiences during the pandemic. While the characters are fictional, the focus on the details of pandemic experiences provides a compelling portrait of what life was like when these fanfictions were written and released. It seems likely that as responses to the COVID-19 pandemic evolve, these fics will take on even more resonance as having being written in a specific time. It will be interesting to determine if pandemic AUs become a popular trope once the actual trauma of the event has receded, much like other historical events become AU settings. Certainly, fanfiction can approach dark subjects; however, pandemic fics written after the pandemic has concluded will necessarily be different than those written during the pandemic. The historicity of this specific type of fic is therefore a productive avenue for future study.

Finally, it is worth considering that the way that fanfiction and fandom operate in this instance is very different from cynical interpretations of fandom as mindless corporate consumerism. Rather, the practice of telling stories about a commonly understood hero and heroine that reflect the experiences of the teller's and the audiences' everyday lives is more akin to traditional folkloric storytelling practices. Previous scholars have used folklore as a way to examine fanfiction (Falzone; Tosenberger), and Ao3's tagging system has been described as a folksonomy (Price); however, scholarship arguing that fanfiction is itself a modern form of folklore—and that recognizes the fruitful contradictions in such a description—is rare. The exceptions can be found in Bacon-Smith's 1992 book *Enterprising Women: Television Fandom and the Creation of Popular Myth* and, albeit with less detail, in Coppa's 2017 *A Fanfiction Reader.* Myths remain an important way that humans make sense of their existence, and never more so than when traumas emerge. Further research is needed to determine how fandom connects to folkloric practices and what insights can be determined about how it functions in that context, particularly when participants experience individual or cultural traumas.

WORKS CITED

Alexander, Jeffrey C., et al. "Towards a theory of cultural trauma." *Cultural trauma and collective identity,* Univ of California Press, 2004, pp. 1-30.

Bacon-Smith, Camille. *Enterprising women: Television fandom and the creation of popular myth,* University of Pennsylvania Press, 1992.

Black, Rebecca, et al. "Representations of autism in online Harry Potter fanfiction." *Journal of Literacy Research,* vol. 51.1, 2019, pp. 30-51.

Brennan, Joseph. "'Fandom is full of pearl clutching old ladies': Nonnies in the online slash closet." *International Journal of Cultural Studies,* vol. 17.4, 2014, pp. 363-380.

Bullard, Julia. "Values and negotiation in classification work." *Proceedings of the companion publication of the 17th ACM conference on Computer supported cooperative work & social computing.* 2014.

Busse, Kristina. "Pon Farr, Mpreg, bonds, and the rise of the Omegaverse." *Fic: Why Fanfiction Is Taking Over the World,* 2013, pp. 316-22.

Busse, Kristina. "Afterword: fannish affect and its aftermath." *Everybody hurts: Transitions, endings, and resurrections in fan cultures,* 2018, pp. 209-218.

Coker, Cait, and Karen Viars. "Welcoming the Dark Side? Exploring Whitelash and Actual Space Nazis in TFA Fanfiction." *NANO: New American Notes Online* vol. 12, 2017, p. 1E.

De Kosnik, Abigail. ""Fifty Shades" and the Archive of Women's Culture." *Cinema Journal,* vol. 54.3, 2015, pp. 116-125.

Duffett, Mark. *Understanding fandom: An introduction to the study of media fan culture.* Bloomsbury Publishing USA, 2013.

Falzone, Paul J. "The final frontier is queer: Aberrancy, archetype and audience generated folklore in K/S slashfiction." *Western folklore,* vol. 64.3/4, 2005, pp. 243-261.

Fiesler, Casey. "Owning the Servers: A Design Fiction Exploring the Transformation of Fandom into 'Our Own.'" *Transformative Works and Cultures* vol. 28, 2018.

Fiesler, Casey, Shannon Morrison, and Amy S. Bruckman. "An archive of their own: A case study of feminist HCI and values in design." *Proceedings of the 2016 CHI conference on human factors in computing systems,* 2016.

Gwenllian Jones, Sara. "The sex lives of cult television characters." *Screen* vol. 43.1, 2002, pp. 79-90.

Hellekson, Karen. "A fannish field of value: Online fan gift culture." *Cinema journal* 48.4 (2009), pp. 113-118.

Hoffman, Matthew. "'Enemies, but complicated enemies': Rey and Kylo Ren's relationship." *Unbound: A Journal of Digital Scholarship* 1.1, 2019.

Holmes, Alyssandra. "Fanfiction as a Form with Merit." *DigitalCommons@University of Nebraska – Lincoln,* 2018.

Horeck, Tanya. "'Netflix and Heal': The Shifting Meanings of Binge-Watching during the COVID-19 Crisis." *Film Quarterly* 75.1 (2021): 35-40.

Jenkins, Henry. *Textual poachers: Television fans and participatory culture.* Routledge, 2012.

Kaplan, Deborah. "Construction of fan fiction character through narrative." *Fan fiction and fan communities in the age of the internet,* 2006, pp. 134-152.

Leavenworth, Maria Lindgren. "The paratext of fan fiction." *Narrative,* vol. 23.1, 2015, pp. 40-60.

Pederson, Joshua. "Speak, trauma: toward a revised understanding of literary trauma theory." *Narrative,* vol. 22.3, 2014, pp. 333-353.

Price, Ludovica. "Fandom, Folksonomies and Creativity: the case of the Archive of Our Own." *The Human Position in an Artificial World: Creativity, Ethics and AI in Conocimiento Organization,* 2019, pp. 11-37.

Schmidt, Lisa. "Monstrous melodrama: Expanding the scope of melodramatic identification to interpret negative fan responses to Supernatural." *Transformative works and cultures,* vol. 4, 2010.

Tosenberger, Catherine. "'Kinda Like the Folklore of Its Day':'Supernatural,' Fairy Tales, and Ostension." *Transformative works and cultures,* vol. 4.1, 2010.

ENDNOTES

1   The longest fanfiction on Archive of Our Own, as of February 2022, was 5,854,121 words long, or just over 1,500 chapters.

2   For those unfamiliar with the terms, mpreg is short for male pregnancy, while omegaverse encompasses a wide variety of fics that occur in a shared universe where characters have sexual roles based on a defined hierarchy drawn from the popular understanding of wolves as alphas, betas, and omegas – hence, omegaverse. For further reading, see Busse's chapter in *Fic: Why Fanfiction is Taking Over the World* (Busse, 2013).

3   Fanfiction has long employed a rating system to ensure that people are not exposed to inappropriate content without consent, from early descriptions of fics as "lemon" or "lime" to indicate pornographic content to Archive of Our Own's current rating system. When a fic is published, it must be tagged as G for general, T for Teen and Up, M for Mature, and E for Explicit. A creator can also opt out of this rating system, which

will indicate to the reader that the author has chosen to do so. In addition, Ao3 offers a separate option to warn for graphic violence, major character death, and underage or non-consensual sex.

4   Holmes references comfort characters in her argument for fanfiction's merit but does little to explore the concept.

Book Review: Leonard's *Protectress*

· ·

Leonard, Kendra Preston. *Protectress.* Unsolicited Press, 2022. 210 pages. ISBN: 978-1950730636

Reviewed by Madison Kooba

As a child, I remember taking any online quiz I could find that would tell me who my Greek-god parent would be, inspired by mythology-influenced characters such as the titular demigod Percy Jackson of the *Percy Jackson* book series. While my growing out of these interests has come with the process of aging, it's also been in part due to recent scholarship that has revealed the damaging traits that typically revered mythological characters uphold. For example, Rachel Smythe's Eisner award-winning webcomic, *Lore Olympus*, depicts the complex drama, gossip, and relationships of Greek gods in a contemporary setting. Though this work might be niche, its recentness and incorporation of such popular and influential mythologies reflects larger efforts of late to reexamine our society's historical prioritization of exclusive and patriarchal ideals, especially as we find ourselves amidst a political climate that has left many people—particularly women—fearing for the safety of themselves and their rights.

It's with this in mind that I say I don't think Kendra Preston Leonard's hybrid poetry-prose novella, *Protectress*, could've arrived at a better time. A retelling of the myth of Medusa, *Protectress* subverts the traditional story of her as a villain who threatened ancient Greek heroes to instead present the tale of her as a once-mortal priestess of Athena who was raped by Poseidon then, cursed by Athena (in an act of victim-blaming) to have snakes for hair and a (literal) stony gaze. Though centering predominantly on a contemporary Medusa who works as a successful college professor, the novella takes place over many centuries as Medusa becomes hardened by an immortal life spent navigating past trauma due to Athena's constant declarations of the supposed *"shame"* (13) she has brought because of her rape.

The first half of the novella focuses on exploring how Athena's mentality—a mentality that many people today adopt towards real-life rape and assault victims—is illogical and incredibly detrimental to the healing and recovery of Medusa, and the real world survivors she stands for, in its juxtaposition of Medusa's experiences as a beloved modern-day professor with the many sleepless nights and nightmares she still suffers in response to Athena's words that have echoed since her rape in Ancient Greece. This heavy emphasis on Athena rather than Poseidon—Medusa's rapist—as the main driver of conflict directs attention to a central theme of *Protectress*, which examines notions of sisterhood to reveal how women's interactions with and expectations of each other can do just as much—if not more—damage than the patriarchal values and hierarchies that they seek to fight against.

Explaining rather than excusing Athena's perspective, Medusa and her sisters' commentary urges the women in their lives to understand that the mere act of being a woman does not mean that one is exempt from upholding oppressive and/or patriarchal ideals: just because Athena is a self-proclaimed female *"warrior"* (82) does not mean that she "represents female agency" and thus, "her womanhood does not make her your ally" (93). This responds to recent movements that desire to call out gender inequality but unintentionally reinforce it, such as statements that have recently circulated on social media declaring that "all men are trash"—an example of misandry rather than feminism, messages such as these curate a womanhood based on exclusion that Preston Leonard subtly but powerfully critiques in her centralization of the novella's conflict in Medusa and Athena's relationship.

Though this serves to condemn the act of women blaming and putting down others, Preston Leonard displays remarkable insight into these perspectives and highlights how they are ultimately the result of a society that has failed both victims of assault and those who blame them for it. As one of Medusa's sisters, Euryale, articulates, Athena's "being the daughter of the world's most / prolific rapist and rape apologist has got / to fuck [her] up" (96), a background which, as Preston Leonard explains, makes "The *shame* she calls for Medusa / … an echo of the shame / her father called for her" (128). Thus emerges *Protectress*'s ultimate argument for a movement "from violence / to serenity" (106) that supports Preston Leonard's notion of sisterhood as rooted in a shared compassion rather than a shared anger. This becomes clear in the second half of the novella, which describes a coming together of Medusa and her sisters with various other mythological women as they, drawing from shared experiences from which they've forged a sisterhood, induct Athena into a space of "welcoming and healing" (114) that they've created to help her recognize how the projections of her own shame and pain have hurt Medusa and other women, in the hopes of establishing a new world in which there are "real sanctuaries / for women, / places of protection, / [and] ways of power" (113) that don't serve to tear each other down.

Not adhering to any formal poetic structure, *Protectress* maintains a fluidity that lends itself well to the rhythmic changes that come with the shifts in environment and emotion, from the tender descriptions of Medusa's "minute, coiled, deli-cate, transparent / baby snake[s]" (15) to the harshness of the italicized and unpunctuated tolling of Athena's "*shame shame shame you should die rather than bear this shame*" (20). This fluidity grants a softness to the novella as well that we find reflected in the attitudes of each character: though all are backgrounded with complex trauma, pain, and anger, a strong sense of sisterhood harbors an intense love shared by the women as they navigate their emotions and experiences together, concluding the novella with themes of rebirth and the hope for "a forward march" (205). I certainly see how this novella, despite perhaps not being the type of text typically utilized in the classroom, can go far beyond a pleasure read to be used as a tool for discussion across multiple disciplines regarding women's rights movements, societal responses to them, and how we can productively move towards a world of unity and support for women.

Book Review:
Kidd's *Pop Culture Freaks*

Kidd, Dustin. *Pop Culture Freaks: Identity, Mass Media, and Society*, 2st ed. Routledge, 2016. 288 pages. ISBN: 978-0813349121.

Reviewed by Carlos Tkacz

In his first chapter, "An Introduction to the Sociology of Popular Culture," of the second edition of *Pop Culture Freaks: Identity, Mass Media, and Society*, author Dustin Kidd writes, "In November 2016, American voters sent popular culture to the White House with the election of Donald J. Trump" (1). Kidd puts it in stronger terms at the end of that chapter: "Pop culture is the 45th president and celebrity studies is the new political science" (30). By beginning what he calls a "field guide" (27) to popular culture studies with the election of President Trump, who managed to leverage his celebrity status into a successful bid for the presidency, Kidd makes a strong case for the importance of popular culture studies in academia. This is a strong version of the student-centered argument that keeping up with popular culture can help teachers engage their students and stronger still than the argument that popular culture influences the identity of individuals in a consumer-based social structure and economy like that of the United States.

Indeed, Kidd's basic idea and the main question the text seeks to answer is the inverse of the latter claim. Rather than asking how popular culture influences identity, he makes clear that he is interested in answering the implied question: how does identity influence popular culture? This flip, while subtle, offers interesting and productive ground for inquiry into the importance and the effects of popular culture in both the American and global contexts that also updates his previous edition (published in 2014) with new examples, more recent data, more inclusive language, and a new chapter. *Pop Culture Freaks,* as such, continues the conversation works like Ray B. Brown's *Against Academia: The History of the Popular Culture Association/American Culture Association and the Popular Culture Movement, 1967-1988* (1989) and Steven Johnson's *Everything Bad is Good for You: How Today's Popular Culture is Actually Making Us Smarter* (2006) began and offers a necessary and perhaps quintessential manual for scholars and students interested in understanding the importance of popular culture in contemporary society.

To these ends, Kidd engages in several overarching themes and concepts that guide his explorations of identity and popular culture, all of which are meant to elucidate on what he calls the "cultural toolkit" (10) that individuals use to make sense of their lives. Fundamental here is the way Kidd breaks up and looks at the concept of identity. While acknowledging the various definitions available to scholars, Kidd chooses to focus on five intersectional aspects of identity: race, class, gender, sexuality, and disability. To understand the influence of each of these on popular culture, which he chose due to their collective natures, Kidd uses the cultural diamond, which he borrows from Wendy Griswold. This conceptual map illustrates the spectrum between creator and receiver and between social world and cultural object. For Kidd, this form allows for more productive inquiries into the complex production, consumption, and effects of popular culture and points towards what he calls the Mass Media Matrix and the Matrix of Identity, both of which are ways of looking at the structures that help to produce media and identity rather than the individual instances of them. These, in turn, lead Kidd to his three main conclusions about popular culture: first, popular culture paradoxically integrates us into the social world while simultaneously telling us we will never fully fit in. Second, the cultural diamond is necessary to understanding the assemblages that make up popular culture. Third, identity influences popular culture through the disparities and inequalities that appear in popular culture, from production to representation.

Each chapter, then, focuses on one of the elements of identity Kidd identifies. The chapters each begin with an exploration of the identity factor in question that includes the necessary theoretical underpinnings necessary for cogent and informed discussion of such difficult topics. Once that is established, each chapter then discusses representations of the chapter's main topic in whatever media formats are applicable, from television and film to sports and social media. From there, consideration is given to the creator (production) and the receiver (audience) sides of the cultural diamond, each followed by information on the methods used to attain and interpret the information presented. Finally, Kidd offers some insight in conclusion and extra resources for continued study. The final two chapters, however, stray some from the above form. Chapter 7, "Translating Harry Potter," looks at the global phenomenon of the *Harry Potter* series of books and films as a way to theorize global popular culture. Kidd focuses on the similarities of global iterations of popular culture and discusses the "McDonaldization" (216), a term he borrows from George Ritzer, of popular culture—the process by which mass media production and consumption both have become avenues through which "culturaleconomic" (217) modes are globally exported and reproduced.

In his conclusion, Kidd writes that "[t]his factory-based

culture industry is doomed to fail" (234) and advocates for "movement from media to art" (236), his way of saying that scholars should and must take popular culture more seriously, especially as technology allows for more and more decentralization in the creative processes that make popular culture. For Kidd, this move leads to a new cultural diamond that puts "participatory creation" across from "changed lives" and "transformed communities" above "revolutionary stories" (236). In the end, it seems, Kidd's book is a defense of the serious study of popular culture, and he manages to make a convincing case in a well-designed and accessible text that also offers scholars and students new and interesting ways of approaching the field. As such, *Pop Culture Freaks* is a necessary introduction and intervention in popular culture studies that is sure to be useful to scholars and students alike.

Author Bios

· · · · · · · · · · · · · · · · · · ·

ARTICLES

Michael Fuchs is a postdoc in the project "Fiction Meets Science" at the University of Oldenburg, Germany. Michael has co-edited six books, most recently *Fantastic Cities: American Urban Spaces in Science Fiction, Fantasy, and Horror* (UP Mississippi, 2022). For more on his past and ongoing research, see www.michael-fuchs.info.

Lisa Funnell is Associate Dean of Creative Industries at Mohawk College.

Shelly Galliah, former writing instructor and current content manager, wrote her dissertation on John Oliver and Jimmy Kimmel's comedic climate change communication. Her interests are popular culture, satire's educational purposes, alternative forms of science communication, data visualization, and online course design. She lives, runs, skis, and walks dogs in Michigan's snowy Upper Peninsula.

Tyler Johnson is Associate Professor of Political Science at the University of Oklahoma.

Anna Marta Marini is a PhD research fellow at the Universidad de Alcalá. Her publications are mostly focused on critical discourse analysis related to violence; representations of border-crossing and borderlands in US popular culture; otherness re/construction in film and comics, particularly in the noir and horror genres.

Kimberly A. Owczarski is an Associate Professor in the Department of Film, Television and Digital Media at Texas Christian University. She has published essays in *Spectator*,

Journal of Film and Video, Quarterly Review of Film and Television, Journal of Popular Culture, Jump Cut, Media Fields Journal and several academic anthologies.

Vicky Pettersen Lantz is an Associate Professor of Theatre and Musical Theatre at Sam Houston State University. Recent publications include "Reimagineering Tourism: Tourist-Performer Style at Disney's Dapper Days" for *The Journal of Popular Culture* and book chapter in *Performance and the Disney Theme Park Experience: The Tourist as Actor.*

BOOK REVIEWS

Madison Kooba is a Master's candidate in English at University of Nevada, Las Vegas. Her primary area of research is in visual literature—particularly comics and graphic novels—and its commentary on various social issues including women's rights and mental health representation. She hopes to pursue a PhD in English to continue studying the intersectionality of literature, visual media, and popular culture, and is currently interested in examining how the films and television shows of the Marvel Cinematic Universe portray women in relation to mental illness and motherhood.

Carlos Tkacz has an M.A. from California State University, Bakersfield and is currently a PhD student at the University of Nevada, Las Vegas, where he studies speculative fiction and pop-culture through an ecocritical lens and in the Global Anglophone context. His particular interests are Native American Literature, science fiction, representations of violence, and narrative theory as it pertains to subjectivity, but he enjoys venturing into critical theory, film studies, comic books, and pretty much anything else when occasion allows.

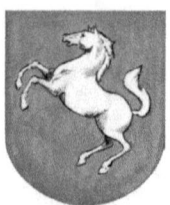

Featured Titles from Westphalia Press

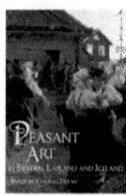

**Peasant Art in Sweden, Lapland and Iceland
by Charles Holme**

This particular work offers a carefully chosen selection of both the decorative and fine arts of Sweden, Iceland, and the northern most region of Finland. A comprehensive survey, it includes paintings, jewelry, textiles, metalwork, carving, furniture and pottery.

**The Rise of the Book Plate: An Exemplative of the Art
by W. G. Bowdoin, Introduction by Henry Blackwel**

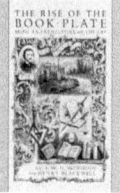

Bookplates were made to denote ownership and hopefully steer the volume back to the rightful shelf if borrowed. They often contained highly stylized writing, drawings, coat of arms, badges or other images of interest to the owner.

**The Art of Table Setting, Ancient and Modern
by Claudia Quigley Murphy**

The arrangement of a table in terms of cutlery, arrangement, serving style, and timing of courses has changed a great deal over time and now is enjoying renewed interest. The History of the Art of Tablesetting was written by a true expert in the field, Claudia Quigley Murphy.

**Thomas Heaphy, 1775-1835, First President of the
Society of British Artists by William T. Whitley**

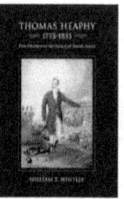

Thomas Heaphy was born into wealth. As such, he was able to pursue his passion of painting snd land development in London. The Society of British Artists was developed by Heaphy, along with 27 other artists, as an alternative to the Royal Academy. It remains in existence today as The Royal Society of British Artists.

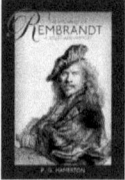

**The Etchings of Rembrandt: A Study and History
by P. G. Hamerton**

Philip Gilbert Hamerton (1834-1894) was an Englishman who was devoted to the arts in numerous forms. Due to the praise, Hamerton stuck with art criticism, and went on to write other works. He also wrote novels, biographies, and reflections on society.

Lankes, His Woodcut Bookplates by Wilbur Macey Stone

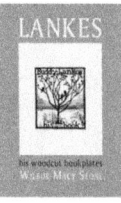

Julius John Lankes was born in Buffalo, New York in 1884, and became a prolific woodcut print artist, as well as an author and professor. As a child, he enjoyed working with the scraps of wood his father brought home from the lumber mill where he was employed. Lankes had a lifelong interest in art.

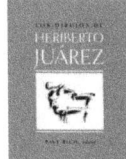

Los Dibujos de Heriberto Juarez / The Drawings of Heriberto Juarez, Edited by Paul Rich

That the drawings here are from life in México is not surprising because Juárez is constantly, and at times impishly, putting art into life and getting art from life. He doesn't think of art as some thing that is done just in a studio or for that matter kept in museums and looked at on Sundays.

The Genesis of Art-Form by George Lansing Raymond

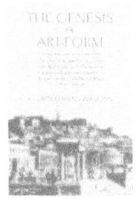

George Raymond became well-known for his writings on esthetic history. He combined psychology, history, art and biology in his theories. He also wrote on ethics, natural law, oration and poetry. His writings were so well received that he was nominated seven times for a Nobel Prize in Literature.

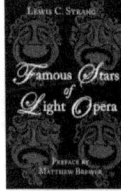

Famous Stars of Light Opera by Lewis C. Strang, Introduction by Matthew Brewer

Strang's attempts to quantify the humorous elements of each performer, as well as quotes from the performers themselves attempting to explain their own success, are an interesting exercise in attempting to explain the inexplicable.

Wood Sculpture: From Ancient Egypt to the End of the Gothic Period by Alfred Maskell F.S.A.

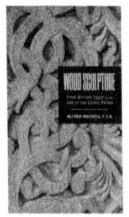

Alfred Maskell was an artist, primarily a photographer, who worked tirelessly to advance the art. Maskell, along with Robert Memachy, helped to develop the gum-bichromate printing, which is able to create a unique painterly image from negatives. This work highlights a variety of wood-based art over time.

westphaliapress.org